# ENGLISH THE AMERICAN WAY:

## A FUN ESL GUIDE TO LANGUAGE AND CULTURE IN THE U.S.

Sheila MacKechnie Murtha, M.A.
Jane Airey O'Connor, M.Ed.

*Research & Education Association*
Visit our website at: www.rea.com

*Research & Education Association*
61 Ethel Road West
Piscataway, New Jersey 08854
E-mail: info@rea.com

## English the American Way: A Fun ESL Guide to Language and Culture in the U.S.

**Published 2015**

Printed in the United States of America

Library of Congress Control Number 2010937924

ISBN-13: 978-0-7386-0676-7
ISBN-10: 0-7386-0676-6

Cover Image © iStockphoto.com/mstay

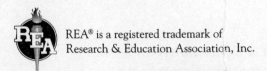

# Table of Contents

# About the Authors

Sheila and Jane have been colleagues and friends for... well, let's just say a long time ☺. As English as a Second Language (ESL) teachers, they worked together on lots of projects... and had lots of fun as they worked. A partnership was born!

Together, Jane and Sheila have teaching credentials in several states and two continents. With years and years... and years... of experience (they just don't want to count them all, ha!), they have taught ESL to little kids, big kids, university students, adults, company executives, and other teachers in the U.S. and Europe (both online and in regular classroom settings).

Both Sheila and Jane have served as members of the New Jersey Department of Education Advisory Committee for ESL/Bilingual Education. They've facilitated online ESL training courses for teachers through the NJ DOE professional development program. Sheila has held several leadership positions scoring teacher candidate responses for an international testing company, and Jane has written ESL test questions and rated English as a Foreign Language exams for another internationally recognized testing company. (They teach, they test, they score!)

They have won many awards for excellence in teaching, including two Teacher of the Year awards, and corporate citations for excellence. They've given numerous presentations and have written curriculum and syllabi for diverse ESL populations. Add to this some fun teaching projects in Spanish, public speaking, drama, writing... and, we're not kidding, even soccer skills (okay, not our finest moment)... and you've got two writers who know how to have a good time writing a book!

Jane is now the Director of ESL Services for Emory College of Arts and Sciences in Atlanta, Georgia. Sheila is a lecturer in the English Language Program at the University of Pennsylvania, and continues to teach, write and consult in New Jersey and New York. Although they live several states away, both are happy to find time to work together on fun projects... like this book!

# A Letter from the Authors

Hi there! Thanks for choosing our book. We think it shows just how smart you are ☺.

We had a lot of fun writing this book, and we hope that you'll have a lot of fun reading it. Well, have fun, but also learn a lot about the English language and American culture.

We've always loved English—the sound of the words, the fun of the idioms, and the interesting way the words work together. We also know that learning all this stuff can be a challenge to English language learners. And that's where our book comes in!

*English the American Way: A Fun ESL Guide to Language and Culture in the U.S.* is your very own ... well, guide, to... yes, American language and culture ☺. You'll find tons (a lot!) of vocabulary, all of it used in real-life ways. We've included tons of informal language—the stuff you really hear every day. And we take a look at American customs—birth to death, and everything in-between!

We hope this book will be a help in your adventure learning English.

Good luck!

*Sheila*     *Jane*

# Authors' Acknowledgments

**Sheila says:** Thanks to Erin, who said, "You really should write a book"; to James, who gave her something to write it with; and, of course, to Jim, who happily mastered the art of the peanut butter and jelly sandwich.

**Jane says:** Thanks to Mum and Dad for always knowing what to say and what to do. (And what *not* to say and what *not* to do!) You are the best! I hope I am as good a parent to Charlotte as you have been to me.

# How This Book Works

This book has 21 units packed with language and culture!

Each unit has a main topic divided into two or three cultural readings. In these readings and the dialogues that follow, you'll find *real* English, not the simplified language you find in most ESL books. The units are full of vocabulary and informal language— tons of idioms, phrasal verbs and slang—bold within the text, then listed at the end of each section with a simple explanation. Listen to the audio for native speaker pronunciation of the dialogues, then pause and repeat to practice!

Look for grammar reminders, idiomatic expressions, culture tips, and fun facts. Oh, and don't forget to check your understanding (and memory ☺) with the special review sections. You'll find them after every three units.

Good luck, and have fun!

# Symbols used in the book:

| | |
|---|---|
| **TIP 1** → | **TIP,** no, not the money kind of tip ☺. These tips are useful things to know. They give special information about things Americans do and say. |
| ⓘ | Look for this symbol ⓘ in our vocabulary lists to find **informal language**. These expressions are used commonly by native speakers, and we'll help you learn the meanings, beyond the actual words themselves. |
| **PRONUNCIATION POINTER** | These **Pronunciation Pointers** help you say words and phrases with American pronunciation. Mp3 audio download available at *www.rea.com/etaw.* |

***Fun Fact!***

**Fun Facts** are sure to bring a smile...
and some wacky informatioh!

Are you *on your toes* (paying attention)? See
if you notice more examples of language tips
we've already discussed.

# About Research & Education Association

Founded in 1959, Research & Education Association (REA) is dedicated to publishing the finest and most effective educational materials—including study guides and test preps—for students in middle school, high school, college, graduate school, and beyond.

Today, REA's wide-ranging catalog is a leading resource for teachers, students, and professionals. Visit *www.rea.com* to see a complete listing of all our titles.

# Acknowledgments

In addition to our authors, we would like to thank Pam Weston, Publisher, for setting the quality standards for production integrity and managing the publication to completion; Larry B. Kling, Vice President, Editorial, for his overall direction; Michael Reynolds, Managing Editor, for project management; Christine Saul, Senior Graphic Artist, for designing our cover; and Stephanie Phelan Design for designing and typesetting this edition.

# New Friends

**Get Started**

## Hi There!

### New country? New friends!
### *But how do you meet them?*

Making new friends is an exciting part of moving to a new place, but sometimes it's hard to know just how formal to be with new people. Americans are usually very **casual**. They're also very friendly. This is a good thing, but it can be **tricky**. Everyone knows that good old basic English phrase, "Hello. It's nice to meet you." Oh, yeah, we bet you were ready for that. Well, you may be ready, but then you may be surprised to learn that you won't hear that phrase very often. "Hello. It's nice to meet you" is okay for first-time introductions, but when friends meet socially, the conversation will probably sound more like this:

**ALAN: Hey**, Lia! It's good to see you.

**LIA:** You, too. I haven't seen you in a few days. How are you? How's it going?

**ALAN**: Not bad. I'm so busy with the classes I'm taking. How about you?

**LIA:** I'm okay. I know you're busy with classes. My job's really **hectic** this time of year, too. What's new with you?

**ALAN:** Nothing much. I'm on my way to the **mall**. I need some **time off**! Do you remember Lana? She's there. Ha! She's always at the mall! I think a lot of our friends plan to just **hang out** at the mall tonight.

**LIA:** Who? Oh yeah. I remember Lana. She's the one with the scary-looking dog. I don't want to hang out with that dog!

**ALAN:** Ha! You aren't afraid of that little tiny dog, are you? Well, I'm sure Rover isn't at the mall.

**LIA:** Actually, I'm **headed** to the mall later, anyway. There's a **huge sale** going on. I think they're open extra late.

**ALAN:** Great! Maybe I'll see you there.

**LIA:** Sounds good. We're both good shoppers! If I get there before you leave, maybe I'll see you. After all, we aren't leaving until we see all the sales. And I'm not leaving until I have some cute new shoes!

 When people ask, "How are you?" they are really just saying, "Hi." This is *not* a good time to talk about your health!

 The mall isn't just for shopping. Many young people go to the mall to **hang around** with friends. In a city, however, the place to be might be *downtown*.

## VOCABULARY

- **casual**: simple, not formal
- ⓘ **hang out** (also hang around): just spend time with friends, with no special activity
- ⓘ **headed**: going
- **hectic**: very busy

- ⓘ **hey:** hi; also a word to get someone's attention
- **huge:** very, very, very big
- **mall:** a large shopping center with stores and restaurants
- **sale:** a short time of lower prices in a store
- **time off:** relaxation time for yourself, away from your work
- ⓘ **tricky:** seems simple, but is a little complicated

## PRONUNCIATION POINTER

- In spoken English, we often drop the *-ing* ending of words. This means that *how's it going* will sound like **how's it goin'**. *Nothing* sounds like **nothin'**.

- Another very common spoken difference is the word *you*, which is usually unstressed and sounds like **yuh**. *How are you doing* will sound like **How yuh doin'**.

## GRAMMAR REMINDER 1: Verb *to be*
## Affirmative Statements and Contractions

Of course, our first grammar reminder just *has* to be about the verb *to be*. It may be a little tricky, but it also may be the most important verb in English.

Most speakers use contractions (the short forms) rather than full forms of the verb in affirmative statements. To really sound like a native speaker, practice, practice, practice using contractions! Notice the contractions of the verb *to be* in the dialogue:
- **I'm** on my way. (I am)
- **You're** busy. (You are)
- **It's** good to see you. (It is)
- **She's** there. (She is)
- **There's** a huge sale. (There is)
- **We're** both good shoppers. (We are)
- **They're** open extra late. (They are)

## GRAMMAR REMINDER 2: Verb *to be*
## Questions and Negatives

For questions using the verb *to be*, put the question word first, then the verb *to be* in its correct form, and then the subject.

**Correct Examples:**
How are you?
What's new with you?

**Not:**
How you are?
What with you is new?

To make a negative, just add *n't* (or *not*) to the form of *to be*. **Isn't** that easy?
**Examples:**
You **aren't** afraid of that little dog.
Rover **isn't** there.
We **aren't** leaving.

## Meet the Neighbors

Although Americans are very friendly, they are also rather private. You may be surprised to know that very often people don't even know their neighbors. In a big city, it's very possible that people living in the same apartment building won't know the people **next door**. In the **suburbs**, it's not unusual for neighbors to wave from their cars or to say "Hi" across their **yards**, but not to know their neighbors' names. Have you noticed how many houses have fences around them? It may seem strange, but it's really just an example of how much Americans **value** a sense of privacy, especially at home. Friendly, but private—now that's tricky! Of course, some neighbors just like to party all the time. Hoo, boy! That can be a problem.

## DIALOGUE 2: TRACK 3

**LIA:** Hi. I'm Lia Chen, your neighbor from around the **block**. We're having a **barbecue** Saturday, and we thought you might like to come. **Lots of** the neighbors will be there. Jae and Ramon are coming, too. They're your neighbors across the street.

**ALAN:** It's nice to meet you, Lia. I'd like to come, but I'll be working all weekend on a big project for my job.

**LIA:** Well, if you **change your mind**, come on over. You're welcome to come, and I think it will be fun for you to meet all the neighbors.

**ALAN:** Thanks. By the way, I've been **meaning to** talk to you. I hope my dog's **barking** doesn't bother you.

**LIA:** Actually, I wanted to talk to you about that. When you're gone during the day, the dog barks all the time. It's **driving me nuts**.

**ALAN:** I'm really sorry! I'll keep the dog in the house when I'm gone.

**LIA:** Thanks so much. I hope you'll come over for some **burgers and dogs** on Saturday. And **drop by** our house to visit anytime!

**TIP 3**

When people are trying to be friendly, they may ask you to "drop by anytime." Don't believe it! This is a way of being friendly, but most people don't like unexpected visitors to drop by. It's always a good idea to call first and ask if the person is busy.

**TIP 4**

If you are invited to a party or barbecue, it's polite to bring something. Before you go you can ask, "What can I bring?" Even if the **host** says, "Nothing," you should bring something. It can be a special food treat from your culture or some flowers. Other kinds of gifts are *not* usually given.

## VOCABULARY

- **barbecue** (also called a cookout): an outside party where food is cooked on a grill
- **barking**: dog talk!
- **block**: in a neighborhood, the area from street to street
- ⓘ **burgers and dogs**: hamburgers and hot dogs
- **change your mind**: make a different decision from your first one
- ⓘ **driving someone nuts** (or **going crazy**): doing something very annoying (or being annoyed)
- ⓘ **drop by**: go to someone's house without an invitation
- **host**: person who invites others to a party
- ⓘ **lots of**: many
- **meaning to do something**: intending or planning to do something
- **next door**: the apartment or house right next to yours
- **suburbs**: neighborhoods just outside the city
- **value**: think something is very important
- **yards**: small gardens around houses

## Fun Fact!

Many neighborhoods have a "block party" during the summer. All the neighbors bring some food and drinks to share, and everyone has a great time.

## Those Crazy Kids! | (Just for fun)

It's probably the same in the country you come from, but teenagers here sometimes sound like they speak a different language. Everyone uses some slang, sometimes, but it seems that **teenagers** use their own slang \*all\* the time! You may not expect to have a conversation like the next one, but you'll probably hear one, and it's fun to know what these **crazy** kids are talking about.

## DIALOGUE 3: TRACK 4

**LIA:** Say! Wassup?

**JAE:** Nothing much. What are you **up to**?

**LIA:** Nothing really. We're just **chillin'**.

**JAE:** Hey, you're really **rocking** those cool jeans! You're really **stylin'**.

**LIA:** Thanks **a bunch**. They're from the mall. There's a huge sale at that cool store we really like. But, hey, I can't talk now. I **gotta run**.

**JAE: Later, dude.**

**LIA:** Catch you later.

**TIP 5** It's fun to know what kids are talking about, but people who aren't teenagers sound funny using this slang. No **kidding**, dude.

**TIP 6** Exclamations are fun! They don't really have a special meaning, but they add excitement to what you're saying. Here are some examples of common American exclamations: Hey! Wow! Yikes! Hoo, boy! Man! Oh, brother! Oh, boy!

# VOCABULARY

ⓘ **a bunch**: a lot, many

ⓘ **chillin'**: just relaxing

ⓘ **crazy**: this can mean insane, but it's often used to mean funny or silly

ⓘ **dude**: guy (man); girls use this to refer to each other, too

ⓘ **gotta run**: I don't have time to talk right now; I have to go

ⓘ **kidding**: joking

ⓘ **later/catch you later**: I'll see you later

ⓘ **rocking**: wearing something well

ⓘ **say!**: a greeting, like *hey!*

ⓘ **stylin'**: looking very fashionable

ⓘ **teenagers**: people from thirteen to nineteen years old

ⓘ **wassup, what're you up to**: What's up? What are you doing? What's going on? What's new? What's happening? These expressions are all ways of saying *Hi, how are you?*

**Did You Spot It?**

Did you notice the contractions of the plural forms for the verb *to be*?
- **We're** just chillin'. (We are)
- **You're** really stylin'. (You are)
- **They're** from the mall. (They are)

## MORE FUN WITH IDIOMATIC EXPRESSIONS: Greetings

- **How's tricks?:** How are things?
  *I haven't seen you in a while.* **How's tricks?**

- **Where have you been hiding?:** Where have you been?
  *Wow, Susan, I haven't seen you in two months?* **Where have you been hiding?**

- **welcome with open arms:** be very happy to see someone.
  *When his sister came home from college, his parents* **welcomed her with open arms.**

- **tied up:** busy
  *Hey, Sara, I'm glad you called! I'd love to join you for coffee, but I'm* **tied up** *until lunchtime.*

- **What's happening?:** What's new?
  *It's good to see you, Marcus.* **What's happening?**

# Getting Around

## Riding the Bus

### No car? No problem!

There are plenty of ways to get around. Most cities and towns have an **efficient mass transit** system; that is, they have buses or trains to get you where you need to go.

Often, you may need to take a bus to the train station. Sometimes it can be **complicated** to figure out which bus or train will take you where, but there is help! Most cities have a special department just to **provide** that information. You can call the transit company to ask. When you call the company, you will need to tell them where you are and where you need to go. You can also ask if you need exact change for the bus. Drivers usually can't accept cash.

## DIALOGUE 1: TRACK 5

**TRANSIT OFFICE:** Good afternoon. Unionville Transit System. This is Stanley speaking.

**COMMUTER:** Hi. I need some travel information. I need to go to 52nd Street and Broadway. I live on 8th Street, near Fifth Avenue.

**TRANSIT OFFICE:** Well, you can take the B12 bus to Mercer Street. Then you'll have to **catch** the B9. You can **take the subway**, too.

**COMMUTER:** I live near a **bus stop**, so I prefer to **take the bus**. What time does it come?

**TRANSIT OFFICE:** The buses **run** about every 15 minutes. Bus schedules are posted at the bus stop. You can also check our website.

**COMMUTER:** How much does it cost?

**TRANSIT OFFICE:** You'll need $2 in change. The driver won't take dollar bills, and he won't give you change. Make sure you have **exact change**.

**COMMUTER:** Okay. Thanks for the help. Have a good day.

**TIP 1**

Most bus systems offer a *transfer*. If you need to take more than one bus to get somewhere, you can get a free transfer to the second bus or train. Ask the driver!

**TIP 2**

Many companies have an 800 number. An 800 number is a telephone number that will not be charged on your phone bill. Yay! We like free phone calls!

## VOCABULARY

- **bus stop**: the place you must go to wait for a bus (They are several blocks apart. They are usually marked with the bus route and have posted schedules.)
- **commuter**: someone who travels to and from work on the bus or train, or by car
- **complicated**: not easy to understand
- **efficient**: smart and fast
- **exact change**: the correct number of coins

- **mass transit**: a transportation system provided by a city
- **provide**: give
- **run**: come, on a schedule
- **subway**: an underground train system
- ⓘ **take/catch the bus or train**: get on a bus or train

## PRONUNCIATION POINTER

- Even though it looks funny when you write it, the word *buses* is pronounced **busses**. In fact, some people spell it with two s's, just like it's pronounced. (Sometimes in English a word may have two correct, but different, spellings or pronunciations.)

- *Have to* sounds like **hafta** in spoken English.

## GRAMMAR REMINDER 1: The Present Simple Tense— Affirmative Statements

The present simple tense is used to talk about things that happen all the time or usually. The verb is used in its base form.

***Don't forget*** to add the letter *s* in the third person (he, she, it)!
### *Examples:*
- I live
- You live
- He, she, or it live**s**
- We live
- They live

## GRAMMAR REMINDER 2: The Present Simple Tense — Negatives, and Questions with *does*

For present simple third-person questions (except that **wacky** verb *to be*), don't forget to use *does* and the *base form* of the verb.

| *Questions — Correct Examples:* | *Not:* |
| --- | --- |
| What time **does** it **come**? | What time does it comes? |
| How much **does** it **cost**? | How much does it costs? |

To form the negative, just add the contraction form of *not* between *does* and the base verb.

- It **doesn't** come late.
- It **doesn't** cost too much.

## GRAMMAR REMINDER 3: The Future Simple Tense
## Affirmative Statements, and Negatives

Use *will* (or the short form/contraction) for the future simple tense when talking about a fact.

- You**'ll have** to catch the B9. (You will have to . . .)
- You**'ll need** $2 in change. (You will need . . .)

Use the short form of *will not* (*won't*) for the negative.

- The driver **won't** take dollar bills and he **won't** take change.

**Stay tuned!** There *will* be more reminders about *will* later on!

## Going Underground: The Subway

Large cities have very efficient subway systems. Taking these trains can get you just about anywhere in the city, and you don't have to wait outside in the rain! At some stations, there may be people singing or playing a musical instrument. This can be an **entertaining** way to wait for the train—unless the singer isn't very good, haha. For most subway systems, you will need a **token** or **farecard**. You can buy these right at the station, either at the **token booth** or at the ticket machine. You can put dollars or credit cards right into the machine. It will give you a farecard in the amount you choose. To get onto the **platform**, slide the card into the card reader or put a token into the slot. Then push through the **turnstile** and **hop on** the train!

## DIALOGUE 2: TRACK 6

**ALAN:** I need some tokens, please.

**TRANSIT WORKER:** One way or **round trip**?

**ALAN:** Round trip. And I'd like a few extra ones, please.

**TRANSIT WORKER:** Most people aren't **crazy about** carrying around a lot of tokens. Maybe you should just get a farecard. It's better than a pocketful of tokens, and you can use it anytime.

**ALAN:** Thanks. That's a good idea. Do I need exact change for a farecard?

**TRANSIT WORKER:** No, the machine can take bills, and it will give you change.

**ALAN:** Thanks for the tip. Now can you tell me where I get the train to Broadway? And where do the trains arrive?

**TRANSIT WORKER:** Sure. Catch the train right over there. Just follow the signs for Northbound/Uptown trains. You'll have to change at 34th Street for the D train.

**ALAN:** Thanks. And can you tell me where the **restroom** is?

**TRANSIT WORKER:** Right over there on the left.

**TIP 3** In some cities like New York City, you can buy a *FunPass*. This is a special farecard that you can use all day. It usually costs about the same as two trips, but you can use it as many times as you like. It's a real bargain!

**TIP 4** Americans rarely ask where the toilet is. Instead they use the word *restroom* or *bathroom*. Careful! These public restrooms are not places to take a rest or a bath! These terms are just polite ways of saying *toilet*.

## VOCABULARY

- ⓘ **crazy about**: really like a lot!
- • **entertaining**: amusing, fun
- • **farecard**: a prepaid card that you can use instead of a token
- ⓘ **hop on**: get on; jump on
- • **platform**: the place in the station beside the train tracks where you wait for your train
- • **restroom**: toilet
- • **round trip**: there and back again!
- ⓘ **stay tuned**: pay attention for more information; don't go away!
- • **token**: used in place of a coin to pay a fare

- **token booth:** a place in the station where you can buy tokens, and where a transit worker can help you
- **turnstile:** a machine that lets people go through one by one
- **wacky:** silly, crazy, complicated

## GRAMMAR REMINDER 4: The Present Simple Tense
## Negatives, and Questions with *do*

For questions using *I, you,* or plural subjects, use *do* and the base form of the verb. To form the negative, just add the contraction form of *not* between *do* and the base verb.

> *Examples:*
> - **Do I need** exact change? (I **don't have** exact change. You **don't need** exact change.)
>
> - Where **do the trains arrive?** (They **don't arrive** on this platform.)

**Usage Reminder:** *I would like* is a more polite way of saying *I want*. It's often shortened to *I'd like*.

## Hey, Taxi!

If the train and bus won't take you where you need to go, or if you're in a hurry, you can call a cab. In larger cities, you can **hail a cab** on the street. Just step off the sidewalk into the street (watch for cars and buses!) and raise your arm. You can also call out, "Taxi!" In cities, the **fares** are posted right in the **cab**, and the **rates** are set by a group that regulates taxi companies.

If you need a ride in a smaller city or town, you can call a car service. This is a private taxi company that usually does not have cars driving around the streets. Drivers wait in the office until someone calls, and then a manager will **dispatch** a car. You can also call **in advance** and **arrange** to be **picked up** on another day.

## DIALOGUE 3: TRACK 7

**CAR SERVICE:** Little Apple Car Service. This is Larry speaking.

**LIA:** Hi. I need a car to take me to the airport at 5:30 p.m. tomorrow.

**CAR SERVICE:** Do you need to be there at 5:30, or is that when you want us to pick you up?

**LIA:** I need to be at the airport at 5:30 or I'll miss my flight.

**CAR SERVICE:** That's right in the middle of **rush hour**. Traffic will be a **nightmare** at that time. I'll have a car get you at 4 p.m. What's your address?

TIP 5

Tipping (everyone loves a tipping tip)! Drivers of buses and trains do not get a tip; however, tipping is expected for taxi drivers. The usual tip is 15% to 20%. There is no extra charge for singing **cabbies**!

## VOCABULARY

- **arrange**: make a plan for something
- **cab**: taxi
- **cabbie**: taxi driver
- **dispatch**: send
- **fare**: the cost of the trip
- **hail a cab**: signal that you want a taxi
- **in advance**: before the time
- **nightmare**: a very bad situation
- **pick up**: get, collect
- **rate**: how the fare is calculated
- **rush hour**: the very busy traffic times (morning and evenings) when most people are traveling to and from work

## MORE FUN WITH IDIOMATIC EXPRESSIONS:
## Transportation

- **off track:** off the subject
  *The meeting got **off track** when Juan began talking about his family's vacation.*

- **lose track:** forget or lose
  *I **lost track** of where I put my glasses. How will I be able to read the paper?*

- **one-track mind:** thinking of only one thing
  *They couldn't make any progress at the meeting because the boss had a **one-track mind** and could only talk about his golf game that afternoon.*

- **miss the boat:** miss an opportunity
  *When the salesman came, he offered all the workers free coffee, but Stephen **missed the boat** because he was chatting on the phone.*

- **in the same boat:** in the same situation
  *They're both **in the same boat**: neither of them remembered to do the homework.*

# Taking a Drive

## Everybody Loves the DMV

Are you **fed up** with **hanging around**, waiting for buses and trains? They go everywhere, but waiting at that bus stop gets pretty **chilly** in the winter. Cabs are really **convenient**, but they sure can be expensive. What's the perfect solution? Drive! I know, I know. You may not have a car. The good news is that it's cheaper to get a license than to get a car. Ha! And although you can't borrow a driver's license, you can rent a car. But watch out for those crazy drivers! You'll need to make sure you know the rules of the road. Each state has all the information and rules about getting a license on its **DMV** website. "DMV" stands for *Division* or *Department of Motor Vehicles*. The **bad news:** there is usually a test!

## DIALOGUE 1: TRACK 8

**LIA:** Hi. I'd like to get a New Jersey driver's license.

**DMV WORKER:** Do you want to **renew** a New Jersey license or **apply** for a new one?

**LIA:** I don't have a New Jersey license, but I have my license from my country.

**DMV WORKER:** You can't use that here. Do you have an application?

**LIA:** No, I don't.

**DMV WORKER:** You'll need to fill out an application. Do you have the **required picture ID?**

**LIA:** Yes, I do and I have my passport. Do I need anything else?

**DMV WORKER:** You can check this list of required documents. If you have all the **paperwork**, you just need to take a **vision test** and the **written test**. When that person is finished, you can go to **booth** number 9 and have your picture taken.

**LIA:** Yikes! Can I **skip** the picture? I'm having a **bad hair day**!

**DMV WORKER:** Sorry. Our state requires a photo-license.

**TIP 1**

Rules for getting your license can be different in each state. Before you go, make sure you check what documents you need. It can be very **frustrating** to wait on line, then find out you don't have the right documents. You can find out on the DMV website when you check the office hours. This is not a place anyone likes to visit more than once!

**TIP 2**

It's a good idea to take a newspaper with you (you can practice reading English). The long lines at the DMV are famous (and not in a good way!). Don't go on a bad hair day. You'll be **stuck with** that license photo for a long time.

## VOCABULARY

- **apply:** to fill out documents asking to get something
- ⓘ **bad hair days:** times you just don't look your best
- ⓘ **bad news:** unpleasant situation

- **booth:** a small space with a table and, sometimes, a computer
- **chilly:** a little bit cold
- **convenient:** easy
- **DMV:** **D**ivision of **M**otor **V**ehicles (Some states may have a slightly different name, but most use Motor Vehicles in the name.)
- ⓘ **fed up** (also **had enough**): tired of something
- **frustrating:** annoying, making you angry or upset
- **GPS:** short for **G**lobal **P**ositioning **S**ystem; the signal from a satellite that shows exactly where you are
- ⓘ **hanging around:** just waiting
- **paperwork:** forms and documents (ugh!) that must be filled out
- **picture ID:** an **I**dentification **D**ocument that shows your photograph
- **renew:** bring your old license up-to-date
- **required:** necessary
- ⓘ **skip:** omit, leave out
- ⓘ **stuck with:** required to keep
- **vision test:** a simple eye test (to be sure you can see that truck behind you!)
- **written test:** a test taken in the DMV office to test driving knowledge; usually taken on a computer

### *Fun Fact!*
Most big city taxi cabs have a **GPS** screen in the back. You can watch the crazy turns as you travel to your destination.

## GRAMMAR REMINDER 1: The Present Simple Tense— Short Answers

To give a short answer to present simple questions, you *don't* repeat the verb. Simply say: *Yes, I do*. Or *No, I don't*. We usually use the contraction in short answers. In the third person use *does* and *doesn't*.

**Examples:**
- Do you have the required picture ID? **Yes, I do.**
- Do you have an application? **No, I don't.**
- Does he have a picture ID? **Yes, he does**.
- Does she have the paperwork? **No, she doesn't.**

*Remember:* The answer will be different with that wacky verb *to be!*

*Examples:*
- Are you a good driver? **Yes, I am.**
- Is he a good driver? **No, he isn't!**

## Let's Go for a Ride!

So you'd like to take the family for a drive in the **country**. A train might take you there, but it's so much easier to **see the sights** by driving around in a car. Maybe it's time to rent a car. It's always a good idea to check many car-rental companies to find the best  price. You can search on the Internet or call the company's 800 number. What kind of car do you want? You'll need to decide on a type: **economy, midsize,** or **luxury**. You can choose the car that fits your needs. Be prepared to pay more for larger cars. You'll also need to buy insurance, just in case a bear in the country decides that your **compact** car is lunch!

## DIALOGUE 2: TRACK 9

**LIA:** Hello. I'd like to **rent** a car for the weekend.

**FRIENDLY RENT-A-CAR:** Do you have your driver's license with you?

**LIA:** Yes, I do.

**FRIENDLY RENT-A-CAR:** If you want an economy car, we have a nice compact outside.

**LIA:** Is it a four-door?

**FRIENDLY RENT-A-CAR:** No, it isn't. It's a two-door, but it has a **hatchback**. And it has a **sunroof**!

**LIA:** Do you have anything bigger and faster?

**FRIENDLY RENT-A-CAR:** Well, we have a midsized **convertible**, but the compact is more economical.

**LIA:** How about a big **van**? I have a large family.

**FRIENDLY RENT-A-CAR:** Sure, we have a van. It's very roomy. It's the biggest and most expensive of the three.

**LIA:** Well, I'd like the convertible for myself, but I guess I'll take the van. Maybe next time…

## VOCABULARY

- ⓘ **bucks:** dollars
- **compact:** the smallest size car
- **convertible:** a car with a special soft roof that folds completely down (Driving with the top down can be great in the summer—not so much fun in the rain!)
- **country:** far from the city, an area of trees and farms
- **damage:** harm or injury to a person or to a car
- **economy:** having to do with saving money
- **hatchback:** a door at the back that lifts up and out for loading
- **luxury:** very special, with extra conveniences
- **midsize:** a medium-sized car, usually with four doors
- **rent:** pay money to use something for a limited time
- ⓘ **see the sights:** visit attractions in a new place
- **sunroof:** a window in the roof of the car that can be opened.  Be careful in the rain!
- **van:** a very large vehicle that can carry up to 12 passengers

## GRAMMAR REMINDER 2: Comparatives

To compare two short adjectives, use the comparative form. Just add the letters -er to the short adjective.

*Examples:*
- A midsized car is **faster**.
- The luxury car is **bigger**. (Note: sometimes the consonant is doubled.)

To compare longer adjectives, use **more**.
*Example:* The smaller car is **more economical** than the van.

Do not use both *more* and -er! Do not say *more faster*.

# GRAMMAR REMINDER 3: Superlatives

To compare three or more things with short adjectives, use the superlative form. Use *the* and the letters *-est*.

**Example:** A midsized car is *the* **fastest**.

To compare three or more things with longer adjectives, use *the* and *most*.

**Example:** The luxury car is **the most comfortable** one of all.

Do not use both *most* and *-est*! Do not say the *most fastest.*

## Oops. Sorry, Officer

Oops. What are those **flashing** lights behind you? Oh, no! Were you careful to watch the speed limit signs along the road? Those flashing lights don't mean a party this time; they mean the police officer would like to have a little **chat** with you. Maybe you shouldn't have rented that fancy car after all.

The flashing lights on a police car usually mean the police officer has noticed a **moving violation**. If a **cop** pulls you over, move to the **shoulder** of the road right away, as safely as you can. Be careful of **traffic** on the highway! It's important to be respectful to the officer, even if you're not sure why he or she is stopping you.

## DIALOGUE 3: TRACK 10

**STATE TROOPER:** Good morning, sir. I **pulled you over** because the speed limit is 50 miles per hour. You were driving much faster than that. You were doing 70.

**ALAN:** I'm sorry, **Officer**. I didn't **notice** the sign, but I thought I was driving slower than that.

**STATE TROOPER:** I need to see your license and **registration**.

**ALAN:** I don't have my license with me. I think I left it home.

**STATE TROOPER:** You need to have license and registration with you in the car at all times, sir. I am going to **issue** you a **ticket** for **speeding** and another one for not having the proper documents. You can call the clerk's office to find out the amount of the **fines**.

**ALAN:** Can I just pay you now?

**STATE TROOPER:** Sir, police officers aren't **allowed** to take money. You have to call the clerk's office. You can go there to pay **in person**, or you can mail it in.

**ALAN:** This is my first speeding ticket.

**STATE TROOPER:** Have a nice day, sir.

 Know what documents you need to keep in your car.

 If a police officer pulls you over, *don't* get out of the car. Wait for the police officer to come to your window.

 Be *polite*. Those police officers have had a **tough** day!

## VOCABULARY

- **allowed:** permitted
- **chat:** a casual conversation
- ⓘ **cop:** police officer
- **fine:** the amount of money you must pay for certain violations
- **flashing:** shining brightly on and off, very quickly
- **in person:** going yourself to do something directly
- **issue:** give out
- **moving violation:** a motor vehicle law that's broken while driving, such as speeding
- **notice:** see
- **Officer:** the respectful title for a policeman or policewoman
- ⓘ **pull over:** move the car to the side of the road
- **registration:** a document showing the owner of a car
- **shoulder:** space on the side of the road, usually marked by a line, where a car can park if there's a problem
- **speeding:** going faster than the speed limit. This is a no no!
- **state trooper:** member of the state police force
- **ticket:** a document showing a road law you've broken; it requires payment of a fine

ⓘ **tough:** difficult

• **traffic:** a lot of cars in the same place on the road

## MORE FUN WITH IDIOMATIC EXPRESSIONS: Cars

• **get a lot of mileage out of something**: be able to use something for a long time
*Even after five years, the sweater looked great. She was happy she **got a lot of mileage out of it.***

• **road hog:** a driver who takes up space in more than one lane on a road
*She knew she would be late when she got stuck driving behind a **road hog** on the way to work.*

• **get the show on the road**: get started with something
*He spent the whole day packing for his trip, and now he just wanted to **get the show on the road.***

• **traffic jam**: many cars stuck on a road without being able to move
*He didn't care about being stuck in the **traffic jam**; he was happy to listen to his new CD.*

• **lemon:** a car (or other item) that continues to have problems even after it's been repaired many times
*He was nervous about buying a used car from a stranger. "With my luck," he said, "I'll get a **lemon.**"*

# Review: Units 1–3

## VOCABULARY

*Fill in the blanks. Use the words below.*

| | | | | |
|---|---|---|---|---|
| sale | apply | rush hour | yard | skip |
| fine | tricky | platform | sunroof | fare |

1. Hey, let's go to the mall today. There's a great _____, so we should be able to get some vacation clothes at a really good price.

2. There's Bob, working in his _____ again. He's always cutting the grass and watering the flowers.

3. The train for New York will depart from _____ number 4.

4. I need to _____ for a New Jersey driver's license.

5. I love a car with a(n) _____ I can open, but my wife complains it messes up her hair and gives her a bad hair day!

6. Dad, can you help me with my math homework? This problem is really _____; I just don't understand it.

7. Let's take the bus; I'm not sure I have enough cash for the taxi _____.

8. The worst time to drive around a city is during _____. There are too many cars and buses crowding the streets.

9. I'm so hungry; I was late getting up this morning and had to _____ breakfast so I wouldn't be late for work.

10. I got stopped by the police for speeding, and now I have to pay a _____ .

## INFORMAL LANGUAGE

*Can you explain these expressions? Try using them in a sentence.*
11. headed
12. drive someone nuts
13. hang around
14. fed up
15. pull over
16. change your mind
17. catch the bus

18. see the sights
19. a nightmare
20. hail a cab

## GRAMMAR

*Choose the correct answer.*

21. Hi, how _____ doing?
    a. you are
    b. are you
    c. you is
    d. is you

22. What time _____ the bus come?
    a. is
    b. do
    c. are
    d. does

23. What time _____ you go to school?
    a. is
    b. does
    c. do
    d. has

24. You'll _____ to take bus number three.
    a. to have
    b. having
    c. have
    d. nothing needed

25. I'm sure it _____ rain tomorrow.
    a. don't
    b. doesn't
    c. won't
    d. isn't

26. Do you like coffee?

    a. Yes, I do.
    b. Yes, I am.
    c. No, I do.
    d. No, I aren't.

27. Does your husband like coffee?

    a. No, he don't.
    b. No, he doesn't.
    c. No, he isn't.
    d. No, he does.

28. It _____ cold near the equator.

    a. isn't
    b. doesn't
    c. don't
    d. won't

29. A luxury car is usually _____ than a compact car.

    a. big
    b. biggest
    c. bigger
    d. more big

30. Many cars are more economical, but a big luxury car is _____ of all for a long drive.

    a. the more comfortable
    b. most comfortable
    c. the comfortablest
    d. the most comfortable

# Dining in Style

Good Food Ahead

## Zipping Through the Drive-Thru

I don't know about you, but I'm **exhausted**! All that waiting for the bus and hailing taxis has made me hungry. Hungry? Yes. **In the mood** to cook? No way! Hmmm. The hard part is deciding where to go and what to eat. Restaurant choices are endless: steaks, **vegetarian** meals, burgers, pizza, and **ethnic cuisine** from just about every country on earth. Even the **picky eaters** will be happy! But I think some **takeout** is **just what the doctor ordered**. There's nothing like fast food after a busy day. Ha—fast food for when you're feeling slow.

But don't let fast food's **bad rap** fool you. It's more than just burgers and fries with a chocolate shake. With people becoming more **health conscious** (and **conscious of** those extra pounds!), restaurants are providing more and more healthy choices: salads, water, lean proteins, and **whole grain** breads. In fact, many restaurants now **post** the calorie counts of their menu items. I'm not sure I want to know that my mega-cheeseburger lunch has more calories than I need for an entire day!

Once you have your **dream** dinner in mind, you can just **hop into** your car and head to the nearest **drive-thru**. Sure, it may seem a little strange telling a machine that you want a mega-burger with cheese, but when you continue to the window to pay, the **cashier** will have your juicy burger order all ready to go. Ah, I can taste the fries already...

## DIALOGUE 1: TRACK 11

**MACHINE GUY:** Can I take your order, please?

**LIA:** Hmmm. A burger sounds good. I think I'll have a mega-burger with cheese, extra pickles, no **mayo**.

**MACHINE GUY:** Anything to drink with that?

**LIA:** I'd like a Coke. Extra large.

**MACHINE GUY:** Anything else?

**LIA:** Yes, a **kids'** meal with chocolate milk and **chicken nuggets**.

**MACHINE GUY:** Would you like fries with that?

**LIA:** Hmmm. The fries smell great, but do you have fruit instead?

**MACHINE GUY:** Sure. You can have an apple or **fruit cup**.

**KID:** Mom, you know I like fruit cup, but I'd like to have the apple. But only if they put a **pie** around it!

Most places will **fix the food to order**. Just ask if you want something a little different from the usual preparation.

Although fast food places offer many choices, don't expect a **gourmet** meal. There's a reason it's called *fast* food!

## VOCABULARY

- ⓘ **bad rap** (also called a **bum rap**): an unfair bad opinion
- **cashier**: the person who takes the money when you buy something
- **chicken nuggets**: small pieces of chicken, covered in a batter and deep fried (come on . . . we know you love them!)
- **conscious of**: aware of, thinking about
- ⓘ **dream**: anything that is just PERFECT! (a dream job, a dream vacation)
- ⓘ **drive-thru**: Yep! a lane outside the restaurant you drive right through; order your food at one end, and pick it up at the other
- **ethnic cuisine**: cooking styles from different cultures

- **exhausted**: really, really tired
- **to fix the food to order**: prepare exactly as you would like it
- **fruit cup**: a serving of mixed fruits
- **gourmet**: very special food, often expensive
- **health conscious**: concerned about things that are good for your health
- ⓘ **hop into**: get into
- ⓘ **in the mood**: wanting to do something
- ⓘ **just what the doctor ordered**: something that will be perfect for what you need
- ⓘ **kids**: children
- ⓘ **mayo**: short for *mayonnaise*, a white spread made from eggs and oil
- ⓘ **picky eaters**: people who don't like many different kinds of food
- **pie**: a pastry treat, usually prepared with fruit
- **post**: show clearly
- **takeout**: pretty much what it says. You buy the food, and take it with you to eat at home
- ⓘ **thru**: a short way to write *through*
- **vegetarian**: without meat products
- **whole grains**: grains (for example, oat and wheat) that are not processed

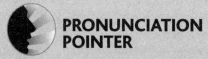

### PRONUNCIATION POINTER

Don't forget to connect your words and phrases like native speakers do. *Hop into* sounds like **hoppinto**.

## GRAMMAR REMINDER 1: Stative Verbs

Some verbs (called stative verbs) are usually only used in the simple form. They refer to states or conditions. Examples of stative verbs are verbs of the senses (for example, *smell* and *taste*) and verbs of feeling (for example, *love*, *like*, *hate*, and *want*).

Can you see the stative verbs in the dialogue above?

- The fries *smell* great.
- I *like* fruit cup.

## GRAMMAR REMINDER 2 : *Would You Like or Do You Like?*

Should you say what *would* you like or what *do* you like?

You remember that *I would (I'd) like* is a more polite way to say what you want than *I want*. However, someone may just want to know, in general, what you like. Then you may hear, "What do you like?" You might answer that, in general, you like something: "I like coffee because it helps me wake up."

If someone asks you what you **would like**, they are asking **what you want** to eat or drink at that moment. If they ask you what **you like**, it is a general question about your preferences.

### Examples:
What **would you like,** tea or coffee?
**I'd like** a coffee, please; I'm feeling really sleepy so I need something to wake me up.

What **do you like**: tea, coffee, or soda?
**I like** coffee best, but the caffeine keeps me awake.

## A Little More Upscale

Maybe you've decided that a table near a window sounds better than a front seat near a **windshield**. It may be time to **splurge** on a nice **dinner out**. It's easy to find a nice **sit-down restaurant** without **breaking the bank**. Especially in a tough economy, restaurants will do almost anything to get your business. Lots of places offer a **Restaurant Week** menu all year. Take advantage of the **early-bird special**. You can have a fancy dinner at a much lower price.

Many restaurants are chain restaurants; this means they have restaurants of the same name and type in many towns or cities. At many places, you can call ahead and make a reservation, and they will save a table for you at a certain time. They'll ask what time you'd like to eat, and how many will be in your **party**. Some restaurants won't take a reservation. For those places, you **check in** at the **hostess station** when you arrive. The hostess will write down your name and call you when a table is **free**. Some very popular restaurants have a very long wait for a table. The hostess may give you a cool little **gadget** to hold while you wait in the bar or outside. When a table becomes available, the gadget buzzes and vibrates and little lights start **flashing**. (This can be very entertaining!) The flashing lights mean that your table is ready. The wait is no fun, but the little gadget sure is.

## DIALOGUE 2: TRACK 12

**SERVER:** Hi. Welcome to the Farkel Family Restaurant. I'll be your **server** today. You're **just in time** for our early-bird special, so you can choose from that menu or from the regular menu. Can I start you off with some **appetizers** and something to drink?

**ALAN:** I think I may have a beer. What do you have **on draft**?

**SERVER:** We have Statler Lite and Orange Cow **on tap**.

**ALAN:** What's your **house wine**?

**SERVER:** The house red is a **Napa Valley** cabernet, and the house white is a chardonnay from Mendoza, Argentina.

**ALAN:** I'll have a glass of cabernet.

**SERVER:** And for you, ma'am?

**LIA:** I'm driving so I'll just have an **OJ**.

**SERVER:** Would you like any appetizers?

**ALAN:** No, I think we'll just have the **entree**. I'll have the **filet mignon**.

**SERVER:** Sure. **How would you like it**?

**ALAN:** I'd like it **rare**. And **hold** the mushrooms.

**SERVER:** And for you, ma'am?

**LIA:** I'll have the **seafood** combination with rice.

**SERVER:** The dinner comes with a vegetable. What would you like?

**ALAN:** I'll have broccoli and a **side salad**.

**LIA:** And I'll have some **sautéed** onions with the seafood.

**TIP 3** Steak is usually prepared to order. If you like your meat very lightly cooked, order it **rare**. More cooked, but still pink is **medium**. Cooked for a longer time with no pink is **well done**.

**TIP 4** A party in a restaurant is not necessarily a birthday party, although it could be. Confused? A *party* is simply the number of people in a group wishing to share the same table.

**TIP 5** The law is very clear: Don't drink and drive! Many people have a "**designated driver**" when they go out. This person will not drink any alcohol, and he or she will be responsible for driving.

## VOCABULARY

- **appetizer**: a small dish of food served before the main meal
- ⓘ **breaking the bank**: costing too much for your budget
- ⓘ **check in**: let the staff know that you would like a table
- **dinner out**: Yes! Eating anywhere but home
- ⓘ **early-bird special**: a lower-cost menu, usually offered before 6 p.m.
- **entrée**: the main meal
- **filet mignon**: a very tender cut of steak
- **flashing**: going on and off very quickly
- **free**: available; can also mean *at no cost*
- **gadget**: a cool little device that has some special use
- ⓘ **hold**: don't include something
- **hostess station**: usually at the front of the restaurant, where the staff will take your name
- **house wine**: the brand of wine a restaurant serves if the customer doesn't want something particular
- **how would you like it?**: how you would like your meat cooked (rare, medium, or well done)
- ⓘ **just in time**: arrived right before it's too late
- **Napa Valley**: a famous wine region in California
- ⓘ **OJ**: Orange Juice
- **on draft, on tap**: pulled from a keg, rather than served in a bottle
- **party**: the people who are joining you for dinner
- **Restaurant Week**: a week when fancy restaurants offer a special menu at lower cost
- **sautéed**: fried quickly in an open pan

- **seafood**: various types of fish
- **server**: also called a *waiter* or *waitress*
- **side salad**: a small salad served with or before the entree
- ⓘ **sit-down restaurant**: a nicer restaurant with tables and waiters who will serve you
- **splurge**: spend a little extra money for a special treat
- **upscale**: a little fancier; more special
- **windshield**: the large front window of a car

## GRAMMAR REMINDER 3: Count/Noncount Nouns

Count nouns (things you can count, for example, one glass, two glasses... you get the idea!) will take the verb that goes with the number. However, noncount nouns (things you can't count, for example, *wine*, *sugar*, and *water*) take a singular verb.

**Note:** *Count* nouns are sometimes called **countable** nouns and **noncount** nouns are sometimes called **uncountable** nouns. It's the same idea, no matter what they're called: some things you can count, and some things you can't!

> *Examples:*
> **Water is** the healthiest beverage. (noncount)
> The **house wine is** delicious. (noncount)
> Some scientists say that **sugar is** not good for your health. (noncount)
> **Two glasses** (of wine) **are** expensive. (count)
> **A cup** (of coffee) **is** a nice dessert. (count)

**Remember:** A noncount noun (for example, *beer, coffee*) acts like a count noun if you put it into a container: a bottle of beer; a cup of coffee. In fact, if you simply say *a beer* or *a coffee*, people will know what you want. See how Lia asks for a *Coke* in dialogue 1 and Alan asks for a *beer* in dialogue 2.

## Is This What I Ordered?

We know what you're thinking: I'm having a **lovely** dinner out, why should I complain? American restaurants place a **top priority** on excellent service. Because people have so many choices when dining out, if a restaurant's service isn't perfect, it can lose customers. The waiters and waitresses know that great service equals great tips, so they'll do their best to be sure you have an excellent meal. But, let's **face it**: everyone has a **bad day**. You may have a **beef about** something if the food or service is not right.

Servers are not surprised if a customer has a **legitimate complaint.** For example, it is **absolutely** unacceptable for anything in the **place setting** to be dirty. Your server should **apologize** and **immediately** replace the item with one that is **spotlessly** clean. Although this is not fast food, if the service is too slow or if the waiter doesn't ask often enough if there's anything you need, then you can complain. If the food is not hot when it arrives, you can complain. If you don't get the dish that you ordered, you can complain. Of course, the best way to complain is to be very polite.

If there has been a problem and if you're polite when you **mention** it, the restaurant staff will usually try their best to **correct** their mistake. There's an expression in English: "You can catch more flies with honey than with vinegar." This means that if you are polite, people will try to make you happy. If you are rude, they may not try their best.

### DIALOGUE 3: TRACK 13

**ALAN:** Miss… Excuse me, but my glass has a **smudge** on it.

**SERVER:** I'm terribly sorry sir. I'll get you a clean one right away.

*** Some time later ***

**ALAN:** Miss, I'm still waiting for a clean glass, and we still haven't received our salads. We've been waiting a long time for our food.

**SERVER:** I am SO sorry! We're a little busier than usual tonight, and we're **short-staffed**. I'll bring it immediately. I'll also bring more water.

*** *A few moments later* ***

**SERVER:** Here you are, sir, and I've brought you another glass of wine, **on the house**. The manager would also like to give you a dessert of your choice, also **compliments of the house**. We're so sorry for the **mix-up**. Sorry you had to wait.

**ALAN:** Thank you very much.

**TIP 6**

A polite way to address a man you don't know is *sir*. Use *ma'am* for a woman.

**TIP 7**

Another tip about tips: You should tip in restaurants. For many servers, tips make up most of their pay. Usually the tip is 15% to 20% of the bill. If the food/service is exceptionally good, you may like to leave a little more.

## PRONUNCIATION POINTER

We get the word *ma'am* from the formal word *madam*. You may never hear the word *madam*, but you will surely hear *ma'am*, pronounced *mam*, as in *dam* or *Sam*.

## VOCABULARY

- **absolutely**: completely
- **apologize**: say you are sorry for something
- **backstroke**: you guessed it… a swimming move done on your back!
- ⓘ **bad day**: a day when you seem to have a lot of problems
- ⓘ **beef about**: complain
- **correct**: fix; to make something right
- ⓘ **face it**: accept the truth
- **immediately**: at once; right away
- **legitimate complaint**: a good reason for mentioning a problem
- **lovely**: very nice
- **mention**: say

- ⓘ **mix-up**: a mistake
- ⓘ **on the house, compliments of the house**: it's FREE!
- **place setting**: dishes, glasses, and silverware on the table
- **server**: waiter or waitress
- **short-staffed**: not enough people working
- **smudge**: a dirty mark
- **spotless**: perfectly clean
- **top priority**: most important

### Fun Fact!
Restaurant jokes are popular. Here's one:
*Customer:* Hey, waiter, what is this fly doing in my soup?
*Waiter:* I think it's doing the **backstroke**!

## GRAMMAR REMINDER 4: More Count/Noncount Nouns

More tips for count/noncount nouns:
Singular count nouns take articles (*a, an, the*). Noncount nouns are usually considered singular, but they do not take articles.

### Example:
- I would like **an** apple. (count)
- I think I'll have **a** glass of beer. (count)
- **The** glass is dirty. (count)
- **Rice** is a good choice with seafood. (noncount)
- **Sugar** is good in coffee. (noncount)

## MORE FUN WITH IDIOMATIC EXPRESSIONS: Food

- **chew the fat:** have a casual conversation
*After the meeting, Tom and Susan stayed a few minutes to **chew the fat**.*

- **in a nutshell:** a summary
*The park ranger gave a very long report about the dangers of forest fires. **In a nutshell**: Be careful with your campfires!*

- **a piece of cake:** easy!
*Lina was so relieved about her driving test. She had expected it to be tricky and hard, but it was **a piece of cake**!*

• **take it with a grain of salt:** don't believe it completely
*Because the study was done by a company that wants to sell the product, people should **take the results with a grain of salt**.*

• **butter someone up:** say nice things to someone to win his or her favor
*Ellen was hoping for a promotion at work, so she tried to **butter up** the boss with compliments about how nice she looked. (But we bet the boss took the compliment with a grain of salt!)*

# Get Moving

Good Times

## Play Ball!

Sometimes it may seem like it, but eating, and waiting for the bus aren't the only fun (!) activities that Americans enjoy. Americans love their sports. They play sports, and they watch sports; their kids play sports, and they watch their kids play sports... you get the idea. **Organized sports** make it easy for adults and children to join local teams and play their favorite sports **competitively**. Local towns have **sign-ups** each season for **various** teams. **Heck**, our husbands think they're superstars of the over-40 soccer team! (They still think they're 21, but that's a topic for another book.) Many companies sponsor teams, and their employees practice and play after work. On weekends, lots of people love to **catch a game**, either on TV or at the **stadium**.

Although Americans enjoy almost every sport, **major league** baseball is often considered the all-American sport. **Couch potatoes** enjoy watching every game on TV. The season's high point is the championship series between the top two professional teams. Yes, even though the teams only come from the U.S. or Canada, the championship is called the World Series.

I guess the baseball "world" is smaller than the real world.

When the seasons change, so do the sports. Soccer (yes, we know the rest of the world calls it *football*) is becoming very popular, and a **pickup game** of basketball is always fun. Some U.S. presidents even **shoot hoops** on the White House basketball court. But in the winter, Americans love their football! (Yes, we know the rest of the world calls it *American football*.) And what could be better than combining two favorites: football and food. The **concession stands** at any sports activity are always crowded. No health food here; the favorites are hot dogs, fries, hot **pretzels**, peanuts, and beer. In fact, the last football game of the season, the Super Bowl, is a hugely popular event with lots of parties and, of course, plenty of **junk food**. Yum!

## DIALOGUE 1: TRACK 14

**LIA:** Wow, look at that guy. **He can really move!**

**ALAN:** What's the **big deal?** I can do that!

**LIA:** Ha! You want me to believe that you can run like a football player?

**ALAN:** You don't think I can? Of course I can! Okay, maybe I can't. But I sure could run when I was in high school. I was a star of the school track team.

**LIA:** Wow, you can remember all the way back to high school? Well, let's just watch the **pros**. Woo hoo! **Touchdown!**

**JAE:** I don't know about anyone here running, but both of you sure can eat. You're **hogging** all the snacks. If you guys don't stop **pigging out**, there won't be any left for the next half. Pass the **nachos**.

**LIA:** Here, **dig in**.

**ALAN:** Not me! I guess that's a **hint** that I should **watch my weight,** haha!

**TIP 1**

During the Super Bowl is the perfect time to go to a restaurant or go shopping. The place will be empty! Everyone will be home watching the game.

## VOCABULARY

ⓘ **big deal**: something important

ⓘ **catch a game**: watch a game

• **competitively**: playing to win

• **concession stand**: place to buy snacks at a game

- ⓘ **couch potato**: someone who prefers to relax and watch TV
- ⓘ **dig in**: eat and enjoy!
- ⓘ **he can really move**: an expression of admiration at someone's ability to run
- ⓘ **heck**: another exclamation; just for fun
- **hint**: a gentle suggestion
- ⓘ **hogging**: keeping most of something for yourself
- ⓘ **junk food**: food that tastes great but isn't good for you (Come on, we know you love it!)
- **major league**: professional baseball; also an idiom meaning "really important"
- **nachos**: a snack of crispy tortilla chips, melted cheese, and salsa
- **organized sports**: local teams that meet on a regular basis
- **pickup game**: an unscheduled, informal game that happens when people just start playing at a park or other place
- ⓘ **pigging out**: eating greedily
- **pretzels**: a popular salty snack, sometimes soft, sometimes crunchy, in a twisted shape
- **pro**: professional sports player
- ⓘ **shoot hoops**: play basketball
- **sign-ups**: when people join a local team
- **stadium**: an arena, or place where a game is played
- **touchdown**: scoring six points in football (Yes, we mean American football!)
- **various**: different
- **watch one's weight**: be careful about diet and avoid gaining extra pounds

## GRAMMAR REMINDER 1: Modal Verbs of Ability – *Can*

*Can* is what we call a modal verb. It's followed by another "regular" verb in its base form (without any other changes made to it). *Can* is used to show (among other things) ability in the present. When you use a modal verb, do not add the letter -*s* on the third-person singular form.

| *Correct Examples:* | *Not:* |
|---|---|
| I can swim/He can swim. | He can**s swim**. |
| I can't swim. | |
| Can you swim? | He can **swims**. |

## Fun Fact!

Some sports events begin with eating contests! (We are not making this up.) People will see who can eat the most hot dogs or chicken wings. (*burp!*)

## GRAMMAR REMINDER 2: Modal Verbs of Ability— *Could*

To express ability (*can*) in the past, we use *could*.

*Examples:*
I **could** play soccer when I was young but I can't anymore.
I **couldn't** swim when I was a kid, but I learned as an adult.
**Could** you keep track of your finances before computers?

## Members Only! Joining a Gym

So you've decided that watching TV sports is fine for Saturday afternoons, but instead of becoming a couch potato, you'd like to do something active to **stay in shape**. Maybe you prefer building muscle strength to improving your **grip** on the snack bowl... If you can't work a sports team into your schedule, you can always join a gym. There you'll find all the fitness equipment you need to **work out**. Most gyms have special pricing plans that allow you to come in as many times as you'd like. You can **do your own thing** or join classes.

You can even get a personal trainer to help with an individual plan. Many gyms even have a pool, and, of course, they all have locker rooms for changing and storing your **stuff**, as well as showers. Believe us: the people sitting next to you on the bus will be very happy you took a shower after your **workout**!

## DIALOGUE 2: TRACK 15

**LARRY:** Hi. Fitness World Gym. Larry speaking. How can I help you?

**LIA:** Yes, I'd like some information on your gym memberships, please.

**LARRY:** Sure. We have two different types of membership: You can **pay as you go**, where you pay $5 every time you want to use the facilities and $5 for every class you attend. Then there's the monthly plan where you pay a **flat rate** of $45 per month. With the monthly plan, you can come in as often as you want and go to as many classes as you want. Both plans require an **annual fee**.

**LIA:** Sounds good. What equipment do you have?

**LARRY:** All the usual stuff. We have a **cardio** room with **treadmills, ellipticals**, all that **kind of stuff**; a weight room with **all sorts of** weight machines and free weights.

**LIA:** What classes can I take?

**LARRY:** We have yoga, pilates, aerobics . . . There's a **whole bunch** of them. **Check out** our website for information on the class schedules.

**LIA:** Is there a pool?

**LARRY:** No, but we do have a sauna, café, and babysitting facilities.

**LIA:** That's great! What about the hours?

**LARRY:** We're open every day from 6 a.m. to 11 p.m. Would you like me to **schedule** a tour for you?

**LIA:** Hey great. Can you **throw in** a free day pass too?

**LARRY:** Sure. **Drop in** anytime, and I'll give you a day pass.

 **Did You Spot It?** There's that polite phrase *I'd like* again.

 **TIP 2** **Lots of** places will give you a free day pass to try out their facilities. Just ask!

TIP 3

When thinking about a gym membership, remember to read the **fine print** in the contract. You may find out that there are penalties if you decide to quit before the contract is over.

## VOCABULARY

- ⓘ **all sorts of**: a variety
- • **annual fee**: a yearly fee in addition to other fees
- • **cardio**: activities geared toward keeping the heart strong
- ⓘ **check out**: look at
- ⓘ **do your own thing**: do something independently, without a group
- • **drop in** (also **drop by**): come in, visit
- • **ellipticals**: exercise machines
- • **fine print**: the small words in a contract that usually contain all the exceptions to the deal
- • **flat rate**: a payment plan where one fee includes all activities
- • **grip**: grasp on an object
- ⓘ **kind of stuff**: things of a similar type
- ⓘ **lots of**: a lot of; many
- • **pay as you go**: a plan where you pay only for what you use
- • **schedule**: make an appointment
- • **stay in shape**: maintain (keep) a healthy body through diet and exercise
- ⓘ **stuff**: things
- ⓘ **throw in**: add something for free
- • **treadmills**: exercise machines
- ⓘ **whole bunch, lots of**: many
- ⓘ **work out** (v.): exercise
- ⓘ **workout** (n.): an exercise session

# Extreme Sports

Are TV sports and fitness workouts still too **tame**? If you have an **adventurous streak**, you'll be able to find something more exciting. In fact, you'll be able to find just about any exciting adventure you can imagine. How about **scuba** diving or sailing? Many rivers are perfect spots for **whitewater rafting** or **tubing** through the **rapids**. There are commercial **operations** where you'll be able to take helicopter flights or rides in a small plane over popular **attractions**. Have you ever thought about a soaring adventure? A **glider** plane will quietly **drift** high over a scenic area. Maybe a ride in a **hot air balloon** at **dawn** is just what you need for a special relaxing experience. For the opposite of relaxation, try **skydiving**—just don't ask us to jump out of that plane with you. In some mountain areas, you'll be able to take a cable car ride to the top of the mountain. And who doesn't want to jump off a bridge? **Bungee jumping** is just the thing. In many forested areas, you'll be able to enjoy a **zipline** above the trees. We don't know about you, but a **nap** on the couch is sounding better and better . . .

## DIALOGUE 3: TRACK 16

**LIA:** Hey, do you guys **feel like** heading up the Delaware River next weekend? The weather should be great, so we'll be able to go canoeing.

**ALAN:** You know me; I'm **up for** anything.

**LIA:** Cool. My brother has a boat on a lake nearby. We'll be able to spend a day on the river and then go waterskiing the next day.

**JAE:** A boat? **Count me out**. I get really seasick.

**LIA:** Oh, don't be such a **chicken**. It's a small boat on a small lake.

**JAE:** Seriously, if it moves on the water, and I'm in it, I will **throw up**!

**ALAN:** Okay, Lia, it looks like it's just you and me for waterskiing. Do you think you'll be able to **handle it**?

**LIA:** What, put two pieces of wood on my feet and **glide** across the water? Of course I can!

**JAE:** Sorry I won't be able to join you, though I bet it will be pretty funny to watch! Maybe I'll just watch a game on TV.

**ALAN:** It's **your loss**! You'll miss seeing your two friends water-ski like pros!

There's a reason some of these are called "extreme" sports. They can be dangerous. Companies that provide the experiences are very serious about safety **precautions**. Always follow the safety rules.

A gift certificate for an adventure experience is a great idea for a special holiday occasion for a very special person.

## VOCABULARY

- **adventurous streak**: the part of your personality that wants excitement
- **attractions**: interesting or fun places to see
- **bungee jumping**: jumping from a very high place, connected only to an elastic cord
- ⓘ **chicken**: a coward; someone who is afraid of something
- ⓘ **count me in**: plan on doing something or being included in something
- ⓘ **count me out**: plan on not doing something or not being included in something
- **dawn**: very early morning before sunrise
- **drift**: float
- ⓘ **feel like**: want to
- **glide**: move easily
- **glider**: a special light plane with no engine that sails on air currents
- ⓘ **handle it**: be able to do something
- **hot air balloon**: a balloon for traveling through the air (A basket holds the people and the balloon is powered by heated air.)
- **nap**: a short sleep
- **operations**: businesses
- **precautions**: things to do to keep safe
- **rapids**: fast-moving parts of a river
- **scuba**: <u>s</u>elf-<u>c</u>ontained <u>u</u>nderwater <u>b</u>reathing <u>a</u>pparatus (for the tank that supplies oxygen); deep sea diving

- **skydiving**: jumping out of a plane for fun! AAAACKKK!!!
- **tame**: calm, easy
- ⓘ **throw up**: a yucky (eeew!) phrase meaning to be sick to your stomach
- **tubing**: going down a river in a special float shaped like a tire tube
- ⓘ **up for**: ready to do something
- **whitewater rafting**: going down a fast-moving river in a special raft
- ⓘ **your loss**: a way of saying you'll be sorry you didn't do something
- **zipline**: a cable connected to pulleys that lets you slide across

## GRAMMAR REMINDER 3: *Will Be Able to* for Future Ability

*Can* expresses ability in the present, and *could* is for the past. For future ability, use *will be able to*.
   ***Examples:***
   **We'll be able to** go canoeing.
   Do you think **you'll be able to** handle it?

*Usage Reminder:* **Feel like** is a really informal way of saying *would like* to do something.
   - Hey, I **feel like** ordering a pizza. Do you want some?
   - Yeah, I **feel like** a pizza, too. Count me in.

## MORE FUN WITH IDIOMATIC EXPRESSIONS: Baseball

Lots of idioms are based on sports. Here are a few common ones from baseball:

- **hit a home run; knock it out of the park**: excel at some task
  *Susan was nervous about performing the song in front of an audience, but she **knocked it out of the park!***

- **the home stretch**: coming to the end of a project
  *After spending all summer on the business proposal, the team was in **the home stretch** by the time the deadline got close.*

- **a ball park figure**: an estimate
  *When they started to plan the party, they didn't know exactly how many people would come, but they had **a ballpark figure**.*

- **throw a curveball**: face an unexpected complication
  *Just when Irina thought she had all the expenses for the trip planned, the airline **threw her a curveball** by charging a fee for her extra suitcase.*

- **cover all the bases:** make sure there are no problems at any part of a project
  *Although she saved her project document on the hard drive of her computer, she decided to **cover all the bases** and save the project to a flash drive too.*

# Get Away from It All

Peace & Quiet

## Day Tripping

You've spent all that time working out and getting into shape. You must be exhausted! It's the perfect time for a vacation. There are vacation options for any style and to **suit any pocket-book**. **Give me** a five-star hotel in a fancy resort. But my **buddy** prefers a small tent and a backpack full of camping gear. (Eeew! Bugs!) Let's take a look at some of the choices.

Maybe you're on a **tight budget**. (Maybe you spent too much for that gym membership!) Or you may have a crazy schedule at work, and you can't take too many days off, but you'd still like some **R&R**. There's a perfect solution, and even a new word to describe it: **staycation**. Instead of going away, you stay right at home and do fun vacation things nearby. These **day trips** can be as much fun as a fancy vacation. Consider a trip to the art museum, or attend a concert. **Pack up the kids**, pack the car, and head to the beach for a day of sun, sand, and **surf**. Places like New York City have ferries you can ride for free. These boats will make you feel like you're on a fancy cruise—well, a fancy cruise without waiters and fancy meals . . . ha! (In New York City, the **ferry** to Staten Island gives you a **spectacular** view of the Statue of Liberty, and it's free!) Feeling seasick? Go to a nearby park where you can enjoy a nature hike through the woods. (Watch out for the **skunks**.) Many local parks have wilderness trails with signs that identify trees, plants, and animals you may see along your walk. For a day that's a bit more expensive, you might try a **kid-friendly** place like the zoo, an amusement park, or a water park. Don't forget the **sunscreen**!

## DIALOGUE 1: TRACK 17

**ALAN:** You have a **sunburn,** Lia. I think you enjoyed your vacation a little too much.

**LIA:** Actually, we just stayed home. We took day trips, and we discovered places we didn't even know about right in the neighborhood. We even visited the zoo. It was great fun!

**ALAN:** Wow! What a great idea. I finished painting the house. It was *not* great fun.

**LIA:** I printed out some new recipes and cooked some interesting ethnic meals, too. After we cleaned up, we walked around the neighborhood and chatted with the neighbors. And one day we traveled to the beach and practiced our beach volleyball skills. I think that's my new favorite sport. The whole week really was a fun staycation.

**TIP 1**

Watch out for **hidden extras** you may not have thought about. You may have to pay to park your car or pay to go on the beach in some places.

**TIP 2**

Depending on how "'wild'" your wilderness trail is, you may have to **keep an eye open** for **critters** and bugs (eeew!). And we don't even want to think about *snakes. AAAACKKKK!*

**TIP 3**

If there's a fun attraction near where you live, look into a season pass. This will allow you to go as many times as you want all year. It's usually a pretty good **deal.**

# VOCABULARY

ⓘ **buddy**: friend

ⓘ **critter**: fun word for small animals

• **day trips**: short trips that last about —you guessed it— a day

ⓘ **deal**: bargain, a good price

• **ferry**: a medium-size or large boat that just goes short hops, back and forth from one place to another

ⓘ **give me**: I prefer

• **hidden extras**: expenses that aren't included in the main cost

ⓘ **keep an eye open**: be alert

• **kid-friendly**: designed to appeal to kids

• **odor**: a bad smell

ⓘ **pack up the kids**: gather the kids and their stuff

ⓘ **R&R**: <u>R</u>est and <u>R</u>elaxation; a vacation

• **skunk**: a small black animal with a white stripe that makes a *terrible* odor when it's frightened

• **spectacular**: wonderful

ⓘ **staycation**: term for a vacation when you stay at home and do local things

• **suit any pocketbook**: be a cost you can afford

• **sunburn**: Ouch! It's that redness of the skin from being in the sun too long

• **sunscreen**: lotion to protect skin from the sun

• **surf**: waves and sea; the beach

ⓘ **tight budget**: not a lot of money to spare

## *(Not Very) Fun Fact!*
If your dog gets sprayed by a skunk (eeew!), giving the dog a bath in tomato juice may remove the **odor**.

# GRAMMAR REMINDER 1: The Past Simple Tense
## Affirmative Statements, Regular Verbs

We love the simple past tense of regular verbs; just add the letters *-ed*. Can you find all the regular verbs in the dialogue?

## Going Wild

You love adventure! You love the **outdoors!** You love cooking hot dogs over an open **campfire!** We have just the vacation for you: camping! Yes, for the **brave soul** who's not afraid of critters, bad weather, and bad food, this is another fun vacation choice. Camping requires a lot of very careful **advance** planning. You'll need to have **gear** for hot weather and cold,

for rain and sunshine, and for grassy fields and rocky **riverbanks**. If you're in the **middle of nowhere**, you'll need to carry your own food for all your meals, pots to cook it in, plates to serve it on, and **utensils** to eat it with. That means a big (and heavy) **knapsack**. You'll also need to carry around your own little hotel—a **tent**—and the equipment to put it up. Don't forget a **sleeping bag.** I'm exhausted just thinking about it! People who love camping say there's nothing as wonderful as sleeping **under the stars.** We don't know about you, but we're thinking that would make us bear **bait**. No, thanks! We don't want a bear to eat us for a snack before we can even eat our own **trail mix**! People tell us that camping can be fun, but we'd rather stay at a fancy hotel.

**LIA:** Our camping trip was sure a surprise.

**ALAN:** Uh-oh. What happened?

**LIA:** Well, it started out fine. We planned the trip carefully and found exactly the right snacks. We packed all our stuff, and we bought **brand-new** hiking boots. We **pitched** our tent right beside a small lake.

**ALAN:** That sounds good.

**LIA:** It sounded good to us, too . . . until we finished our hike the first day. We forgot to **break in** the new boots! Our feet were sore and **blistered**. Then we noticed the big black clouds, and disaster struck! It **poured** all night. When we woke up in the morning, the tent was collapsed around us, and we were lying in a huge **puddle**.

**ALAN:** Ha, ha! I guess next time you'll stay in a hotel!

| TIP 4 |  | Don't **overpack**! Remember you'll be **toting** that stuff for the whole trip! |
| TIP 5 |  | It's very important to be careful with campfires. Thousands of acres of a World Heritage Site National Park in Chile burned when a tourist was careless with a campfire. |
| TIP 6 |  | If you bring it in, bring it out! Don't leave any trash where you camp. |

## VOCABULARY

- **advance**: before you go
- **bait**: a food attraction for animals
- **blister**: a sore on the foot from rubbing against a new shoe
- **brand-new**: very new
- **brave soul**: someone who is not afraid
- ⓘ **break in**: wear a bit to make them softer
- **campfire**: a small fire made from sticks and leaves
- **gear**: equipment; stuff you need
- **knapsack**: a large backpack

- ⓘ **middle of nowhere**: a remote place far from any towns
- **outdoors**: woods, fields, wilderness; outside
- **overpack**: put too much stuff in your bag
- **pitched**: put up
- **pour**: rain very hard
- **puddle**: pool of water left by the rain
- **riverbanks**: the sides of rivers
- **sleeping bag**: a padded blanket that zips around the body for sleeping
- **tent**: a portable shelter made of cloth
- **tote**: carry
- **trail mix**: a special high-energy snack with fruit, grains, and nuts
- **under the stars**: outside
- **utensils**: cutlery: knives, spoons, and forks

## Fancy-Schmancy

Now we're talking about our favorite vacation! Camping is fun if you like sleeping in a tent. In the rain. With bugs. But give us a **high-class resort** any day! These can be very expensive, but they're fun to dream about even if we can't go. The **amenities** at a **five-star** resort can make you feel like **royalty**, so even if the weather is bad, you'll have a great time. An **all-inclusive** resort is perfect if you **can't be bothered** keeping track of your expenses. The price includes all meals, drinks, and entertainment. Golf or tennis, the **fitness center**, and children's activities are also included. The rooms are often larger, with **king-sized** beds. Some places have all **suites**, so you can really **spread out**. And the hotel usually has a **concierge** who can arrange many extra **excursions** in the local area, like **chartering** a boat to go deep-sea fishing, or planning a **parasailing** adventure. Be aware that these excursions are not included in the cost. Other amenities that may not be included are the **spa**, a **salon**, and other trips to nearby attractions. Be sure to know in advance exactly what fun activities are included. The **downside** to an all-inclusive plan is that you may decide not to explore the local town restaurants. After all, you've already paid for your meals at the hotel. **On the other hand**, if you're **in heaven**, who wants to leave anyway?

**ALAN:** Wow, we had a great time on vacation!

**LIA:** Yeah, Susan told me you went to a really cool place.

**ALAN:** Yeah, it was an **awesome**, all-inclusive resort. We paid for the hotel, and everything we wanted to do was included.

**LIA**: Tell me more.

**ALAN**: Well, the kids spent lots of time in the **arcade**. Susan and I were happy because they had a beautiful golf course. And of course we spent hours on the beach. It was heaven—just sitting in beach chairs and watching the ocean.

**LIA:** What about water sports?

**ALAN:** Oh, it was so cool! We dove for shells one day and water-skied another day. The camp **counselors** taught the kids how to make paper boats—they thought it was awesome! We even brought some little boats home for **souvenirs**.

**LIA:** Wow. You were busy.

**ALAN:** Yeah, we sure were! But I think we ate and drank a little too much. It's time for a diet.

**TIP 7** Check to see if the **gratuity** is included in the cost. Tips could be a hidden extra!

**TIP 8** You can request **in advance** the type of bed you'd like. A room will usually have either one king-sized bed or two **queen-sized**. You can request a **roll-away cot** if you need an extra bed for the kids.

## VOCABULARY

- **all-inclusive**: (almost) all activities and food are included in the price
- **amenities**: things the hotel provides
- **arcade**: a special area for games and prizes
- ⓘ **awesome**: great! fantastic! fabulous!
- ⓘ **can't be bothered**: not wanting to waste time doing something
- **chartering**: renting a boat or bus for a special trip

- **concierge**: a worker in a fancy hotel who helps you make plans
- **counselor**: a person in charge of fun activities at a camp
- ⓘ **downside**: disadvantage
- **excursion**: special trip
- **fancy**: a little extra special, nicer than usual
- **fancy-schmancy**: funny way to describe something fancy
- **fitness center** (also called a **gym**): a place to exercise
- **five-star**: top rated
- **gratuity**: tip
- ⓘ **high-class**: deluxe, very special
- **in advance**: before you go
- ⓘ **in heaven**: in a perfect situation
- **king-sized**: an extra-large bed
- **on the other hand**: thinking about the other side of an issue
- **parasailing**: soaring in a parachute that is pulled by a fast boat
- **queen-sized**: a large bed (smaller than a king)
- **resort**: a special hotel with restaurants and fancy attractions
- **roll-away cot**: a small bed that can be brought into a hotel room
- **royalty**: kings and queens
- **salon**: a business providing hair and nail care services
- **souvenir**: something special you buy to remind you of your vacation
- **spa**: a place for massages and skin treatments; a sauna; a steam bath
- ⓘ **spread out**: enjoy lots of extra space
- **suite**: a small group of rooms

## GRAMMAR REMINDER 2: The Past Simple Tense
### Affirmative Statements, Irregular Verbs

Maybe they aren't so lovable or easy, but "irregular" past tense verbs aren't so bad, once you practice with them. How many irregular past tense verbs can you spot in the dialogue? (See appendix B for a list of some commonly used irregular verbs.)

# MORE FUN WITH IDIOMATIC EXPRESSIONS: Vacations

- **a happy camper**: content with a situation
  *When Michael heard that he could leave work early, he was **a happy camper.***

- **the boonies**: a very rural (country) location, far away from everything
  *They loved the city, so they were not happy campers when they had to move to **the boonies**.*

- **travel light**: pack very few things when you travel
  *Because they knew they'd need space in the car for gifts, they decided to **travel light** and bring only one suitcase.*

- **on vacation**: away from work
  *She couldn't get an answer about her application because the boss was **on vacation**.*

- **a last resort**: a last choice
  *He tried to contact the company by letter, phone, and e-mail. As **a last resort**, he went to the office in person.*

# Review: Units 4–6

## VOCABULARY

*Fill in the blanks. Use the words below.*

| | | | | |
|---|---|---|---|---|
| cashier | gourmet | sunburn | sunscreen | dawn |
| gadget | couch potato | spotless | vegetarian | party |

1. I don't eat meat. I'm a(n) _____.

2. Can you see where the _____ is? I need to pay for this.

3. I'd like to invite Tom over for a meal but he's a _____ chef. I'd be embarrassed by my simple cooking style.

4. Welcome to The Happy Apple Restaurant. How many people are in your _____?

5. My husband has a _____ for everything! His little devices help him do just about everything, from cooking to fixing things. (I just wish he'd put them away when he's finished!)

6. I see you've cleaned the house for our visitors tomorrow. It is _____. Great job!

7. I'm a real _____. I hate exercising but I love watching it on TV.

8. I'm the total opposite. I get up at _____ every morning to go for a run.

9. Don't forget to put on _____ if you are going out in this hot sun!

10. If you lie on the beach without suntan lotion, you could get a bad _____.

## INFORMAL LANGUAGE

*Match the expressions to their meanings. Try using them in a sentence.*

11. break the bank          a. content with a situation

12. beef about something    b. watch a game

13. catch a game            c. do something independently, without a group

14. a piece of cake         d. cost too much for your budget

15. dig in                  e. pack very few things when you travel

16. stay in shape           f. really easy

17. do your own thing       g. maintain a healthy body through diet and exercise

18. keep an eye open        h. be alert

19. a happy camper          i. complain

20. travel light            j. eat and enjoy

## GRAMMAR

Look at the following sentences.

✓ *Put a check next to the sentences that are correct.*

✗ *Put an X next to the sentences that are not correct. Can you underline the error and explain why it's wrong?*

21. Wow, this burger is smelling great.

22. What would you like: tea or coffee?
    I like coffee.

23. Do you like coffee?
    Yes, I really like coffee, but the caffeine keeps me awake.

24. Wine is expensive.

25. Two glasses of wine is very expensive.

26. A rice is a good choice with seafood.

27. He cans swim well.

28. I can played soccer well when I was younger.

29. It was cloudy all day yesterday, and then it poured last night.

30. I loved my teacher in first grade. She teached me many wonderful things.

# Home Sweet Home

## To Buy or Not to Buy; That Is the Question

Deciding on a place to live isn't always easy. Although the traditional American Dream has **typically** included buying a house with a yard and a **white picket fence**, world economies don't always **consider** traditional dreams. People need to **weigh their options** when deciding whether to rent an apartment or buy a house. There are many things to consider, and both **options** have their **pros and cons**.

Probably the biggest advantage to renting is **flexibility**. Although you'll need to sign a **lease agreement**, this can be for a **short term**—sometimes less than a year—which is **handy** if you think you may be **relocating** soon. Remember to read the fine print on that contract! It will probably include rules about keeping pets and how much **advance notice** you need to give the landlord before you move out. You'll need to put down a **security deposit**, which is usually **equivalent** to one month's rent. Sometimes **utilities** are included in the rent, but you may need to pay those separately. Very often the utility companies will charge a **hookup** fee. Of course, **you're on**

**your own** if you want cable TV and high-speed Internet connections.

A big consideration for renters is parking. You're usually **out of luck** if you choose a big apartment building in a city. However, some apartment complexes in the suburbs provide parking areas. Be careful: this could be a hidden extra. The biggest advantage to renting is that if anything goes wrong, you're **off the hook**—it's the landlord's responsibility to fix it!

Buying a house is always a **tempting** choice. The **upside** is that instead of paying money to a landlord each month, you pay off the mortgage and own your own home. Of course, the **downside** is that you'll need a big **chunk of change** for a **down payment**. In addition, you'll need to pay closing costs and **realtor** fees, as well as buying homeowners insurance. Is renting starting to look better and better to you? Most towns have rules about what you may do with your **lot**. For example, you'll need to get a permit to put up a fence, and there are rules about how high the fence can be, and where on the **property line** it must go.

And let's not forget what American **Founding Father** Benjamin Franklin said: "In this world nothing is certain but death and taxes." Ah yes, another good reason to rent: no property taxes! Although towns provide convenient services like trash collection and **recreation**, they get the money for these services from a homeowner's property taxes.

## DIALOGUE 1: TRACK 20

**ALAN:** Hey, Lia, what did you think about the apartment you looked at this morning?

**LIA:** Oh, boy. I was **pretty** disappointed.

**ALAN:** Really? I'm surprised. I thought you'd love the neighborhood.

**LIA:** Yeah, that was the upside. The neighborhood is away from the city, so the yard was beautiful. But here's the downside: there wasn't a subway anywhere near the place! It would **take forever** to get to work.

**ALAN:** Could you take a bus?

**LIA:** It wasn't on the bus route that goes to my office. And besides, there weren't any **appliances**. The building had a laundry room in the basement, but I really wanted one in the apartment. And I couldn't believe it didn't even have a microwave! How would I **zap** my popcorn every night?

**ALAN:** You could always rent appliances or even buy them **secondhand**.

**LIA:** I guess so. But anyway, it had only one bedroom. We have three kids, so that's just not enough space. There were just too many downsides for me to rent that place.

**ALAN:** What's that old proverb? "If at first you don't succeed, try, try again." I guess you'll just have to keep looking to find your dream apartment.

**Chores** are small household tasks done in the home. These include doing laundry, washing dishes, cleaning, and taking out the trash.

**Errands** are tasks that are done outside the house. These are things like going to the bank, going grocery shopping, going to the post office, and going to the dry cleaner.

## VOCABULARY

- **advance notice**: telling someone about something before you do it
- **appliances**: large machines for household chores
- ⓘ **chunk of change**: a large amount of money
- **consider**: think about
- **down payment**: the money required to begin the buying process
- ⓘ **downside**: disadvantage; con
- **equivalent**: about the same as
- **flexibility**: ability to change easily
- **Founding Fathers**: the men who formed the country and wrote the Constitution of the United States
- ⓘ **handy**: convenient
- **hookup**: connection
- **lease agreement**: a rental contract
- **lot**: the property
- ⓘ **off the hook**: not held responsible for something
- **options**: choices
- ⓘ **out of luck**: don't have a chance
- **pretty**: as an adjective this means *attractive*; as an adverb, it means *rather* or *quite*
- **property line**: boundary
- **pros and cons**: advantages and disadvantages

- **realtor**: person whose business is to help people buy and sell homes
- **recreation**: activities for fun and relaxation
- **relocating**: moving
- **secondhand**: used items that can be purchased inexpensively
- **security deposit**: money kept in an account in case the apartment is damaged
- **short term**: for a small amount of time
- ⓘ **take forever**: take a very long time
- **tempting**: makes you want something
- **typically**: usually
- ⓘ **upside**: advantage; pro
- **utilities**: electric, water, gas, and cable
- **weigh one's options**: think about choices
- **white picket fence**: a painted wooden fence with small slats
- ⓘ **you're on your own**: it's your responsibility
- ⓘ **zap** (also *nuke*): cook in a microwave oven

## PRONUNCIATION POINTER

Remember to join your phrases. Prepositions are not usually stressed. *Chunk of change* will sound like **chunka change**. *Out of luck* will sound like **outta luck**.

## GRAMMAR REMINDER 1: The Past Simple Tense— Negatives, Verb *to be*

To form the negative past simple of the verb *to be*, use *was* or *were* and *not*. Remember that most speakers will use the contraction. Look at these examples from the dialogue.

*Examples:*
There **wasn't** a subway anywhere near the place!
There **weren't** any appliances.

# City Life or the 'Burbs

Before you **settle down** in any new place, you need to take a look at your **lifestyle**. Are you a **city person**? Do you like to be **within walking distance** of everything you need? If you enjoy a quick walk down the block to buy a newspaper and coffee, and you like being with lots of people, then **urban** life may be for you. The upside of life in the city is convenience. It's nice to be close to all the things you enjoy: museums, shopping, movies, libraries . . . and work. And the mass transit system in a city makes it simple to get around.

On the other hand, life in the suburbs is often part of the white-picket-fence American Dream. Suburbs are areas just outside the city where homes are usually larger, and there's more **open space**. Instead of stores within walking distance, there are shopping malls you drive to. Homes often have large yards for flower and vegetable gardens. Many houses have **patios** to enjoy outdoor living.

Apartments in the suburbs are usually larger, too, and there are often areas for playgrounds, parking, and cooking out. Suburbs where there are many commuters who travel to jobs in the city are sometimes called "bedroom communities." People work in the urban areas, but they return to their suburban homes to sleep. The upside of suburban life is the space and privacy from nearby neighbors. The downside is that people often need a car to get around.

If you *really* want to **get away from it all**, you may decide that life in the **country** is for you. Picture the **rolling hills** and miles of farmland. Listen to the sounds of birds. Ahh, **peace and quiet**! But unless milking cows is your idea of the dream job, you may want to think carefully about living in the country.

## DIALOGUE 2: TRACK 21

**ALAN:** Lia, since that apartment in the 'burbs wasn't what you're looking for, have you thought about trying to find a place a little closer to the city?

**LIA:** I really think that's what I need to do. The suburbs are beautiful, but there wasn't one store nearby. The kids couldn't easily walk to a friend's house—we'd have to arrange **play dates**. And I think getting to work would be a huge **headache**.

**ALAN:** Yeah, the city really is great for kids to make lots of friends. They just walk outside! We didn't worry about play dates when I grew up in a big city.

**LIA:** It would be nice to have a big garden, but there are too many downsides to the suburbs.

**ALAN:** I think you've decided already. You're a city person!

**LIA:** Yeah, I think I am.

**ALAN:** I guess this means you haven't thought about life in the country with **mooing** cows and **clucking** chickens?

**LIA:** Well, you never know what kind of neighbors you'll have in a big city apartment!

**TIP 3** Because kids in the suburbs often can't walk to a friend's house, their parents arrange a **specific** day and time for a visit. It's considered polite to take turns hosting the kids: One week it's her turn, at her house; the next week it's your turn, at your house. (We know which one we prefer!)

**TIP 4** Each language has its own way to describe the sounds that animals make. In English, *onomatopoeia* is the term used for writing a word that is the sound it makes (for example, *cluck*, *moo*, and *buzz*).

## VOCABULARY

- ⓘ **'burbs**: suburbs
- ⓘ **city person**: someone who is most comfortable in a city
- • **country**: an area with farms, few homes, and lots of open space
- ⓘ **get away from it all**: leave responsibilities and relax
- ⓘ **headache**: something complicated and annoying
- • **lifestyle**: the way people choose to spend their time
- • **mooing** and **clucking**: sounds made by cows and chickens, respectively
- • **open space**: land in its natural state
- • **patio**: an area outside a house, often paved, for relaxing
- ⓘ **peace and quiet**: a calm environment
- • **play date**: an arranged play time for children
- • **rolling hills**: an area of small hills and fields

- ⓘ **settle down**: become established, start a new normal life
- **specific**: exact
- **urban**: having to do with the city
- **within walking distance**: easy to walk to

## GRAMMAR REMINDER 2: The Past Simple Tense — Negatives, Regular Verbs

To form simple past negatives of regular verbs, use the verb in its base form (no changes) and add *didn't*. Remember: *don't* put the letters *-ed* on the end of the verb for the negative. Look at these examples from the dialogues.

| *Correct Example:* | *Not:* |
| --- | --- |
| We **didn't worry** about play dates. | We **didn't worried** about play dates. |
| It **didn't** even **have** a microwave. | It **didn't** even **had** a microwave. |

## Nothing but Bills!

No matter where you decide to live, one thing is certain: you'll be paying bills—lots of bills. Big bills and little bills. Bills, bills, bills! The mailboxes may look different, but what's inside is the same everywhere. If you're lucky, there will be some fun mail—a letter or card from a friend far away. But if you're like most Americans, you'll be opening . . . bills!

It's great to move to a beautiful new place, but everything has a cost. In English we have a saying: "There's no such thing as a free lunch." You'll need to pay for gas, electricity, water, telephone, Internet connection, and cable or satellite television service. It seems the list of bills goes on and on.

Most companies send a bill every month. It's important to pay **on time**— late payments can affect your **credit rating**. Most places encourage you to pay bills online. That means less paper (and less mail). And although a landlord is responsible for repairs in an apartment, as a proud new homeowner, you'll have the fun of paying those expenses for your new house.

Don't forget the **dreaded Murphy's Law**! Sometimes it just seems that everything is on a **timer** to break at the same time. One poor homeowner moved in one year, and the next year the washer, dryer, stove, and dishwasher didn't work. That's Murphy's Law! (Some days we're just happy to get **junk mail**.)

**LIA:** Anything interesting in the mail?

**ALAN:** Just the usual: junk mail and bills, bills, bills!

**LIA:** Uh-oh.

**ALAN:** What's up?

**LIA:** The credit card bill was **due** yesterday . . . and I didn't pay it.

**ALAN:** Don't worry about it. You still have a **grace period** before you get **slapped with** a **late fee**.

**LIA:** I guess so. But I may need to buy a car next year. I want to make sure my credit rating is good.

**ALAN:** You shouldn't have a problem if you pay it right away. Ha ha—I didn't think you'd need a timer to remind yourself about bills!

**TIP 5**

When people move into a new home, they often have a **housewarming** party. Friends will bring a gift for the house as a way to wish the new homeowner good luck.

**TIP 6**

You can remove your name from junk mail lists by sending a letter to the Direct Marketing Association. Don't fill out contest entry forms at the mall. Often these are just tricks to get new addresses!

## VOCABULARY

- **bill:** a statement of how much money you owe
- **credit rating** (also called a **credit score**): an evaluation of how good your credit is, based on your payments
- **dreaded:** worrisome, not wanted
- **due:** expected (and sometimes required)
- **grace period:** a time period after the due date when you can pay a bill without a penalty
- ⓘ **junk mail:** advertising and papers that you haven't requested
- **late fee:** money the company charges if you don't pay on time
- ⓘ **Murphy's Law:** a famous saying: "Anything that *can* go wrong, *will* go wrong."

- **on time**: when it's due; not late
- ⓘ **slapped with**: charged for
- **timer**: a small device that buzzes after a set time has gone by.

### *Fun Fact!*
Okay, we admit it. There are no fun facts about bills!

## GRAMMAR REMINDER 3: The Past Simple Tense— Negatives, Irregular Verbs

To form simple past negatives of irregular verbs, use the verb in its base form (no changes) and add *didn't*. Remember: don't make any changes to the main verb. Look at these examples from the dialogue.

| *Correct Examples:* | *Not* |
|---|---|
| I **didn't pay** it. | I **didn't paid** it. |
| I **didn't think** you'd need a timer. | I **didn't thought** you'd need a timer. |

## MORE FUN WITH IDIOMATIC EXPRESSIONS: The House

- **on the house**: something given for free by a restaurant
  *When the waiter realized it was my birthday, he said dessert was* ***on the house***.

- **hit the roof**: get really angry
  *Lauren* ***hit the roof*** *when she found out her brother borrowed the car without asking her.*

- **drive someone up the wall**: drive someone nuts/crazy
  *The Smiths make noise late at night. Their parties* ***drive the neighbors up the wall***.

- **bring down the house**: have an audience become very excited
  *It was a good concert from the beginning, but when the band played its biggest hit, they* ***brought down the house***.

- **go through the roof**: become very high in value
  *When the new mall was built in town, prices of homes* ***went through the roof***.

# Ooh, Money, Money!

Road to Riches

## Stash the Cash! | Get Started with Banking

Okay, you've found a place to live and a job that will pay the bills. As all the money comes rolling in, you'll need a safe place to save it. A bank account is important for establishing a credit rating, too. You'll also need an account if you want **direct deposit** from your employer. It's easy to open a bank account, and the people at the bank will be happy to help. (Of course they will;  they'll be holding your money!) Speaking to a **representative** at the bank is a good idea because there are so many types of accounts. Do you want to share a **joint account** with someone in your family? Do you want a **checking** account, so that you can pay for things by check? Do you want a savings account to **put aside** extra money? You can usually earn a little more **interest** with a **CD**, which is short for "certificate of deposit." To open an account, you'll need to provide ID and proof of your address. (You got that apartment just in time!)

Here's another time when you need to watch for hidden **fees**. Some accounts may require you to **maintain** a **minimum balance**. If the **funds** in the account fall below a certain level, you may have to pay a monthly fee.

Some "free checking" accounts can be very expensive! Most banks offer free use of their **ATM**s, but be careful of the **double whammy**! If you use a different bank's ATM, *that* bank may charge a fee, and *your* bank may charge *another* fee. (Are you doing the math with me? That's *two* fees!) If your account is **overdrawn**—you guessed it—a fee! If you **bounce a check**—say it with me—a fee! I guess there's a reason banks have enough money to name so many sports arenas . . .

The convenience of having a bank account makes it worthwhile to learn about all the options. Most bank cards can be used at stores (so you don't have to carry cash), and you can even get **cash back** from your purchase. Many banks have drive-thru banking, so you don't even have to get out of your car. Hmm . . . drive thru the bank, and then head to the burger drive-thru for lunch? Lots of Americans love online banking, so you can have fun paying those bills **24-7**, even in your **PJs**!

## DIALOGUE 1: TRACK 23

**LIA:** I finally did it. I opened a bank account yesterday.

**ALAN: It's about time**! Didn't you hate carrying all that cash around?

**LIA:** Yeah, it was a **hassle**. And I want to establish a credit rating, too. Besides, with all the ATMs around, it's easy to get cash if I want some.

**ALAN:** Was it easy to open an account?

**LIA:** It sure was! I guess they're happy to get my money, ha, ha. Just make sure you have ID with you and proof of **residence**.

**ALAN:** Were the people nice?

**LIA:** Yeah, they were pretty friendly. I felt very comfortable asking questions.

**ALAN:** So now that you have a bank account, I guess you'll be buying a new car?

**LIA:** Don't **get carried away**! I'll be happy if I can pay the electric bill!

**TIP 1**

Banking is big business. Check around. Different banks may offer different interest rates to get your business. There are also Internet-only banks that are sometimes a **good deal**.

# VOCABULARY

- ⓘ **24-7**: 24 hours a day, 7 days a week; always open
- **ATM**: <u>A</u>utomated <u>T</u>eller <u>M</u>achine
- **balance**: the amount of money in your account
- ⓘ **bounce a check**: write a check when there isn't enough money in the account
- **cash back**: with certain bank cards, you can pay and get extra money back from your account at a store
- **CD**: <u>C</u>ertificate of <u>D</u>eposit
- **checking**: an account that comes with checks to pay for things
- **direct deposit**: system that allows your company to put your pay right into your bank account
- ⓘ **double whammy**: two problems at the same time
- **fees**: costs
- **funds**: money, usually in an account
- ⓘ **get carried away**: get too excited
- ⓘ **good deal**: a plan with many advantages
- ⓘ **hassle**: a problem; a complicated situation; a "headache"
- **interest**: the amount of money the bank pays you to hold your account funds
- ⓘ **it's about time**: we've waited a long time for this!
- **joint account**: an account that more than one person can access (use)
- **maintain**: keep
- **minimum**: the least amount
- **overdrawn**: you have taken out more money than you actually have in the account
- ⓘ **PJs**: <u>P</u>a<u>J</u>amas (night clothes)
- ⓘ **put aside**: save
- **representative**: someone who works for the company, whose job it is to help you
- **residence**: where you live
- ⓘ **stash**: put away for future use

## PRONUNCIATION POINTER

*Was* is pronounced differently, depending on the stress. Unstressed, it sounds like **wuz** and is connected to the words around it: **Wuz** it easy to open an account? (unstressed)

In its stressed form, it sounds like **woz**: It sure **woz**. (stressed)

## GRAMMAR REMINDER 1: The Past Simple Tense — Questions, Verb *to be*

For past simple questions using the verb *to be*, the question word comes first (if you are using one). The past form of the verb *to be* comes next, *before* the subject. Look at the examples from the dialogue.

*Examples:*
**Were** the people nice? (**How were** the people?)
**Was** it easy to open an account?

## Making the Big Bucks

Place to live? **Check!** New job? Check! And now for the best part: the paycheck! The long **lines** at the bank's drive-thru will tell you that Friday is the traditional **payday**. But you can **outsmart** the people in line. Most companies offer direct deposit of paychecks. This means that your money is automatically transferred into your bank account on payday. Direct deposit has many advantages, but the best one is that you don't have to wait in line to **cash your check**. Yay! (You've probably noticed that Americans don't like to wait.) It also gives you extra time for yourself; you don't have to add a trip to the bank to your list of errands.

Now that you're **bringing home the bacon**, you know that American money **takes some getting used to**. The **bills** look very similar in size and color. The **change** comes in a lot of **denominations**.

You also need to learn the many common slang words that refer to money. Moolah, dough, bread, **cabbage,** and **lettuce** are not referring to a meal, but to the money that buys the meal! The slang descriptions of money may leave you thinking you're learning a third language! One dollar bills are often called singles. Occasionally, a five-dollar bill is called a fin and a ten dollar bill is a ten-spot. The real fun, however, comes with the **big bills.** A **C-note** is a one hundred dollar bill. (We'd like several of those, please. ☺) Although some money nicknames seem to **make no sense**, this one is logical: the Roman numeral for 100 is C. American Founding Father Benjamin Franklin has made it into the slang world, too. A one hundred dollar bill (featuring Franklin's picture) is also called a Benjamin. How are your math skills? Ten Benjamins equal a **grand**. We love those **G**s. That's a lot of **smackers**!

## DIALOGUE 2: TRACK 24

**LIA:** I really love my new job! It feels great to be bringing home the bacon!

**ALAN: No kidding**. Payday is my favorite day. Too bad it only comes twice a month.

**LIA:** Don't you get paid every week?

**ALAN:** No, twice a month. In fact, I think most companies do **payroll** twice a month; usually on the 15th and the 30th.

**LIA:** Hey, I think you're right. But I have direct deposit, so all I care about is that when I pay a bill, there's money in the bank! And I'm saving for a car, so I like that the money is already in the bank.

**ALAN:** Wow—a car? Won't that cost a **fortune**?

**LIA:** You're not kidding. I was looking at used cars, and even they cost at least 5**K**. It's crazy!

**ALAN: Speaking of** crazy . . . I'm still trying to figure out the crazy change here. I know that four **quarters** equal a dollar. But did you ever notice that a **nickel** is bigger than a **dime**? Does that make sense to you?

**LIA:** Ha! Now that you mention it, a **penny** is bigger than a dime, too.

**ALAN:** I learned an interesting fact the other day. Did you know it costs more to make a penny at the **mint** than it's worth? Crazy!

**LIA:** I guess it's fun to think about change, but I'm glad my paycheck is in big bills!

## VOCABULARY

- **big bills**: large denominations of money
- ⓘ **big bucks**: a lot of money
- **bills**: paper money
- ⓘ **bringing home the bacon**: earning a salary
- ⓘ **cabbage, lettuce**: green leafy vegetables; also, slang for *money*
- **cash your check**: get real money for the company check
- **change**: coins; also, the money you get back when you pay with a big bill
- ⓘ **check**: done; completed; a mark on a list to indicate you have finished a task
- ⓘ **C-note**: a one hundred dollar bill
- **denominations**: values
- **dime**: ten cents
- ⓘ **fortune**: a really high price; a lot of money
- ⓘ **grand**: a thousand dollars
- ⓘ **Gs**: thousands
- ⓘ **K**: one thousand
- **line**: a queue; people standing in turn
- **make no sense**: not seem logical
- **mint**: the place where money is made
- **nickel**: five cents
- ⓘ **no kidding**: another way to say *I agree*
- **outsmart**: be more clever than
- **payday**: the day your employer pays you for your work
- **payroll**: the money to be paid to employees
- **penny**: one cent

- **quarter**: twenty-five cents
- ⓘ **smackers**: money
- **speaking of**: while we're talking about the subject
- **take some getting used to**: need to become accustomed to

## *Fun Fact!*

American bills are green. Cabbage is green. Lettuce is green. Some money slang makes sense (or is it "cents" ha ha)! . . .

## GRAMMAR REMINDER 2: The Past Simple Tense— Questions, Regular and Irregular Verbs

For past simple questions using both regular and irregular verbs, the question word comes first (if you are using one). *Did* comes next, then the subject and the base form of the verb. Remember: the word *did* shows that the question is in the past, so the verb does *not* need to change.

*Correct Examples:*
**What** did you notice?
Did you notice?
**How** did you know?
Did you know?

*Not:*
What did you notic**ed**?
Did you notic**ed**?
How did you **knew**?
Did you **knew**?

## MORE FUN WITH IDIOMATIC EXPRESSIONS: Money

- **have money to burn**: have a lot of extra money
  *Since she got her new job, she spends like she **has money to burn**!*

- **pay through the nose**: pay a lot for something
  *You'll **pay through the nose** if you go to that fancy new restaurant.*

- **break the bank**: be so expensive that it costs almost all you have
  *Karen searched the Internet to find a vacation that wouldn't **break the bank**.*

- **feel/look like a million bucks**: feel/look great
  *When Lily's boss loved her project, she **felt like a million bucks**.*
  *So she bought a new dress, and she **looked like a million bucks**.*

- **make a mint**: make a lot of money
  *The kids **made a mint** selling lemonade on a hot day.*

# Shop 'til You Drop!

## It's All at the Mall

Okay, raise your hand if you love shopping. What? No men? In the American **stereotype**, women love spending a day shopping at the mall, while men sit **glumly** on a bench, holding the bags. (And we thank them for that. ☺) A large mall is a shopper's dream come true; there are **specialty stores** for everything! There are stores for kids and stores for kitchens; stores for makeup and stores for men; bookstores and shoe stores and toy stores and **drugstores** . . . well, you get the idea. Malls have at least one **anchor department store.** This is the place to head if you prefer shopping for everything in one store. These large stores **carry** everything from clothing to **housewares.** Want to smell like a million bucks? Stop at the perfume counter for a free **sample** of your favorite fragrance. And that's the **main** advantage of a department store or big indoor shopping mall—you can shop for everything in one place. There are no worries about bad weather. Even your car can stay dry and warm in the mall parking garage! (Raise your hand if you've ever lost your car in a parking garage. "But I was so *sure* I parked right . . . here . . . .")

Although the large, **enclosed malls** bring people from all over, the suburbs also have smaller, local malls. These **strip malls** usually have convenience shops where people can take care of their errands. The stores are lined up next to each other, and the front doors open onto an outdoor walkway. Strip malls usually have a small takeout restaurant, a dry cleaner, a bank **branch**, and a drugstore. Parking is right in front of the stores, so people can hop out quickly and **run in** for what they need. In bad weather this may not be fun, but it's much quicker than parking in a large garage at the mall. And it's easier to find your car!

## DIALOGUE 1: TRACK 25

**LIA:** Hey, look outside. Very bad weather . . . very good mall day!

**ALAN:** No! Not the mall! Anything but the mall!

**LIA:** Calm down. You won't have to go into every store with me. I just want to do some **window-shopping**. Besides, the sporting goods store is having a great sale on sports equipment. You might find the tennis racket you've been looking for. Look at this **ad** from the paper: "Super sale! Many rackets to choose from!"

**ALAN:** Yeah. I really do need a new tennis racket. Okay, if I go, how much time will we have to spend there? I'd like to watch the game this afternoon.

**LIA:** We don't have to stay very long. There are a few things I'd like to look at in the department store, so that will take less time than walking around the whole mall.

**ALAN:** Going to the sporting goods store is a great idea. Actually, if there aren't too many stores you plan to visit, then I don't **mind** going with you. In fact, maybe we could stop at a **big box store** on the way home. I could use some garden supplies.

**LIA:** Sure! If we make a day of it, we could have lunch at the **food court**.

**ALAN:** I'd rather stop at the strip mall in town and get fried chicken takeout.

**LIA:** If you come with me to the mall, we can have anything you want for lunch!

**TIP 1**

Shopping malls have a customer service area where you can get information about the stores in the mall. They have **strollers** to rent and, at holiday times, offer gift wrapping of your purchases. You can also buy **gift cards** at customer service.

# VOCABULARY

- ⓘ **ad**: short for *advertisement*; information about an item for sale
- • **anchor store**: a large store at a mall to attract many shoppers
- ⓘ **big box store**: huge warehouse-type store (There are home supplies stores and electronics stores, among others.)
- • **branch**: an office of a large company or bank
- • **carry**: keep in stock; offer for sale
- • **department store**: a very large store with many departments or sections that offer different types of merchandise
- • **drugstore**: pharmacy (You can get prescriptions for medicine filled here, but you can also buy many other general and personal items.)
- • **enclosed mall**: a center with many stores and inside walkways
- • **food court**: the area of a shopping mall where the fast food shops are located
- • **gift card**: a prepaid card that works like a credit card (When a person uses the gift card for a purchase, the amount is deducted from the balance.)
- ⓘ **glum**: unhappy
- • **housewares**: items for the home
- • **main**: most important
- • **mind**: object to
- ⓘ **run in**: go into a store quickly for just an item or two
- • **sample**: a small size of an item to try. Free! No cost!
- • **souvenir**: a special purchase of something to remember your visit
- • **specialty store**: a store that carries just one kind of merchandise
- • **stereotype**: a belief that may not be accurate about an entire group of people
- • **strip mall**: a line of shops along a street
- • **stroller**: small carriage or cart you can use so small children don't have to walk
- ⓘ **window-shopping**: looking at things in stores, but not buying anything (yeah, right, haha).

## Fun Fact!

In Washington, D.C., the Mall is the large, grassy open area from the U.S. Capitol Building to the Lincoln Memorial. Besides some of the most important museums in the country, there's shopping here, too, with vendors selling **souvenirs**.

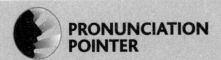
## GRAMMAR REMINDER 1: Expressions of Quantity— *much, many; few, less*

• Use *many* and *how many* for count nouns. Use *much* and *how much* for noncount nouns. *See Unit 4 for explanation of count/noncount nouns.*

• Use *few* for count nouns; use *less* for noncount. Look at the examples from the dialogue.

*Examples:*
**Count**
"Super sale! **Many** rackets to choose from!"
There are a **few** things I'd like to look at in the department store . . .

**Noncount**
**How much** time will we have to spend there?
That will take **less** time than walking around the whole mall.

## Food, Glorious Food!

**Recreational** shopping at the mall is one thing, but basic **grocery** shopping is a **fact of life**. There are many choices when it comes to buying food. The largest and most convenient place to shop for food is the supermarket. At these huge stores, you can find plenty of choices for whatever item you need. Need peanut butter? You can find **creamy** or **crunchy**, **reduced** fat or reduced salt, natural style or processed, small jar or large, with jam or without. Each **aisle** offers great practice for developing your decision-making skills! And to help you decide, the store will often have a **sampling station** where you can taste (for free!) many of the special products they sell. This is usually done on a weekend when lots of people are in the store. "If you try it, maybe you'll buy it!" It's a great way to introduce you to new products, but remember they are just samples! The store expects customers to try only one. (Okay, maybe two . . . ) But if you do it right, you can visit every sampling station in the store, and you won't need lunch when you get home!

Despite all the choices at a big supermarket, however, **farmers' markets** are also very popular. As people become more and more conscious of where their food is coming from and how it's grown, farmers' markets offer an opportunity to buy directly from the farmers who are **on the spot** to answer any questions. Often the markets are set up in public squares in large and small cities, usually on weekends. At the market, local area farmers bring in their **produce** and arrange it on tables for sale. Home bakers will offer fresh-baked cakes and pies made with **homegrown** fruit. There are people selling **homemade jams**, too. Lots of vendors will offer samples of their goods. They may have small squares of bread and small pieces of cheese for you to try. There may be plates of cookies or samples of jams. The **vendors** hope that you'll enjoy the sample so much that you'll buy some to take home. And why not? Although baked goods and produce from the farmers' market may cost more, they're delicious and fresh from the farm!

## DIALOGUE 2: TRACK 26

**LIA:** Do you have any peaches today?

**FARMER:** Oh, boy! I have lots of peaches! The weather has been great for peaches this year. They got plenty of sun and a lot of rain when they needed it.

**LIA:** Ha! I guess that's why there are so many peach pies for sale. They look delicious!

**FARMER:** Several people have **mentioned** that. My wife will appreciate the **compliment**. She baked them.

**LIA:** I'll definitely take a couple of pies. I'm going to a neighbor's barbecue this afternoon, and I want to bring something special for dessert.

**FARMER:** Well, I have some nice organic **herbs**, too. And the corn on the cob is really sweet this year. We can **husk** it here for you, if you like.

**LIA:** I'm so glad your vegetables are **organic**. I've been trying to be careful about the foods I feed my family. I've decided that I'll buy only organically grown produce whenever I can.

**FARMER:** I've been farming organically for 10 years now. No **pesticides**. No **artificial fertilizers**. Just pure nature!

**LIA:** Great! I'll take two peach pies, a **dozen ears of corn**, and some **basil** for **pesto**. I'm making myself hungry already!

**TIP 2** → Farmers' markets are also good places to find **crafts**. People who make **quilts**, special soaps, or little toys often have a space at the market to sell their things. Fun!

## VOCABULARY

- **aisle**: the walkways in the store with shelves of items on both sides
- **artificial**: human-made, not natural
- **basil**: an herb
- **compliment**: something nice or admiring that is said about someone or that person's handiwork.
- **crafts**: special decorations or things that are made by hand
- **creamy**: smooth
- **crunchy**: with bits of nuts
- **dozen**: twelve
- **ears of corn**: corn still on the cob (base)
- ⓘ **fact of life**: something you can't avoid
- **farmers' market**: fresh produce market
- **fertilizer**: a substance to make plants grow better
- **glorious**: wonderful, fabulous, really good.
- **groceries**: food items
- **herb**: a plant used for flavor in cooking
- **homegrown**: not grown on a large commercial farm
- **homemade**: not commercially made; made by hand
- **husk** (also **shuck**): remove the outer leaves
- **jam**: jelly made from fruit
- **mentioned**: said
- ⓘ **on the spot**: right there
- **organic**: no chemicals, all-natural
- **pesticide**: chemicals used to kill insects
- **pesto**: a sauce made from basil, garlic, oil, cheese, and pine nuts. Yum!

- **produce**: farm-grown fruits and vegetables
- **quilts**: thick blankets with beautiful designs made by hand from small pieces of cloth
- **recreational**: for fun
- **reduced**: less
- **sampling station**: a place in shops where a person offers you a free taste of a product
- **vendor**: someone selling an item

### *Fun Farm Fact!*

Three U.S. states have produce nicknames. Georgia is called *The Peach State*. New Jersey is called *The Garden State*. Nebraska is called *The Cornhusker State*. It's a pretty big country to have only three farm nicknames!

## Saving Some Dough

Everyone loves a **bargain**! There's something exciting about buying what you need and want, but saving money while you buy is even more exciting! Businesses know this, and they use a lot of creative ways to attract customers who want to save money. Stores know that if they want to sell something to make room for newer stuff, they should have a sale. The older items are "**on sale**!" Department stores have one-day-only sales and **doorbusters**. Grocery stores put **coupons** in the local newspaper or online, or they send them through the mail. (This is junk mail we can use!) Coupons can save a lot of cash. For example, if a store has a certain item on sale, you get it at a reduced price. If you also have a coupon for that item, you get the sale price, plus the extra money off. Woo, hoo! Time for a vacation with all that extra moolah! But you need to read the coupons carefully. They usually have an **expiration date**, and they may only be good for certain sizes or flavors of a product. Some of these sales are so great that everyone wants to take advantage of the savings. When this happens, a store may **run out** of an item. *Aaackkk!!!* But it's not bad news. Stores don't want unhappy customers, so if something is sold out, they'll offer a **rain check**.

Stores and food companies aren't the only ones who want to attract customers with bargains. Lots of appliance and electronics **manufacturers** will offer **rebates** on **big ticket items**. With this plan, you pay the full price, but if you mail in lots of forms and **receipts**, you'll get some money back. It's nice to save the money, but sometimes rebates can be a hassle. You need to follow the instructions exactly and send in a special form or enter it online. If you lose a receipt, or if you send in the wrong number from the box, you won't get your money back. But if you do follow all the directions, and you mail everything in by the **deadline**, the manufacturer will send you a check for the rebate amount. The upside of a rebate is that it's always nice to get money in the mail with all of those bills, bills, bills!

## DIALOGUE 3: TRACK 27

**LIA:** Hey, how do you like my new shoes?

**JAE:** They're awesome! Where did you get them?

**LIA:** I got them at Shoe City. They're having a great sale. It's **BOGO**.

**JAE:** Who's Bogo?

**LIA:** Ha! BOGO isn't a person! It's a really cool sale. You **b**uy **o**ne **g**et **o**ne. In other words, if you buy one pair of shoes, you get one pair free!

**JAE:** Wow, that's a **steal**! I think Shoe City is at the strip mall in town, and I have a 15% off coupon for the pizza store there.

**LIA:** Let's go shopping!

**JAE:** And let's eat!

**TIP 3**

Sometimes a group of sale items says "as marked." This means that the discount has already been taken. Other times you will get the discount when you pay for the item at the register. Be sure to read the signs.

**TIP 4**

The price on the ticket is not the exact final price. In most states, you'll need to add sales tax to the total. Each state has a different rule on this: Delaware has no-tax shopping; New Jersey has no tax on clothing. See you in Delaware!

# VOCABULARY

ⓘ **bargain**: a very good price

ⓘ **big ticket item**: a very expensive item

• **coupon**: a form offering money off the price of certain items

• **deadline**: last day something will be accepted

• **doorbusters**: special huge sales on certain items to attract a lot of shoppers

• **expiration date**: the date a coupon must be used by, or it won't be accepted

• **manufacturer**: maker of something

• **on sale**: at a special low price

• **rain check**: a form that allows you to get the special price when the item becomes available again

• **rebate**: money back after you have purchased something

• **receipt**: the form that says how much you paid for something and when you bought it

ⓘ **run out**: use up; have no more left

ⓘ **steal**: a great price; often the cost is less than the item is actually worth

# GRAMMAR REMINDER 2: More Expressions of Quantity!

**Expressions of Quantity for Count Nouns**
A couple of peaches
Several peaches
A few peaches

**Expressions of Quantity for Noncount nouns**
A little rice

**Expression of Quantity That Work for Both**
Some peaches/rice
Most peaches/rice
Lots of peaches/rice
A lot of peaches/rice
Plenty of peaches/rice

**Look at the examples from dialogue 2:**
I have **lots of** peaches!
They got **plenty of** sun and **a lot of** rain when they needed it.
**Several** people have mentioned that.
I'll definitely take **a couple of** pies.
Well, I have **some** nice organic herbs, too.

## MORE FUN WITH IDIOMATIC EXPRESSIONS: Shopping

- **like a bull in a china shop**: very clumsy; likely to break things
  *Her husband felt **like a bull in a china shop** when he dropped and broke a glass in the restaurant.*

- **go window-shopping**: look at things in the stores without buying
  *She was saving her money for a new car, so they just **went window-shopping** at the mall.*

- **a steal**: a very good price
  *She only planned to go window-shopping, but the shoes were **a steal** at the sale price, so she bought them.*

- **shop around**: compare prices at many different places
  *A computer is a big purchase, so she decided to **shop around** before she bought one.*

- **talk shop**: talk about work when you're not at work
  *Because their husbands worked at the same office, the wives always went into the kitchen when the guys started to **talk shop** in the other room.*

# Review: Units 7–9

## VOCABULARY

*Match the words to their meanings.*

1. rain check
2. appliances
3. settle down
4. stereotype
5. direct deposit
6. stroller
7. bargain
8. denominations
9. junk mail
10. relocating

a. values of money

b. a very good price

c. advertising and papers that come in your mail (that you never asked for)

d. small carriage or cart for small children

e. become established, start a new life

f. a form that allows you to buy an item at a special price when it becomes available again

g. moving your home and work

h. a belief (that may not be accurate) about a group of people

i. system that allows your company to deposit your pay directly into your bank account

j. large machines for household chores

*Now fill in the blanks using the words above.*

11. Hi Tom. It looks like you're selling your house.
    Yes, we're _____ to Florida for my job.
    How exciting!

12. Angie, I hear you're getting married!
    Yes, I decided it was time to _____ .
    Congratulations.

13. Washing machines, dryers, and stoves are all types of _____ .

14. Anything interesting in the mail today?
    No, just the usual _____ . It can all go straight into the trash can.

15. Do you get paid by check?
    No, I prefer _____ . Then the money goes straight into my bank account.

16. I'd like to withdraw $200 from my bank account.
    Is it okay in two $100 bills?
    No, thanks. I'd prefer different _____ . Can you give me five $20 bills and ten $10 bills?

17. Are all doctors in the United States men?
    No, that's a(n) _____ . There are plenty of women doctors.

18. It's a lovely day. Let's put the baby in the _____ and go for a walk in the park.

19. Look, there's a sale at my favorite store. Maybe if we go early, we'll get some great _____ .

20. Hi, I see you've sold out of the chicken that's on sale. Can I get a _____ so I can buy it next time I'm here?

## INFORMAL LANGUAGE

*Look at how these expressions are used in a sentence. Can you explain what they mean?*

21. I'm sorry Alfredo, but you're **out of luck.** You can't have a day off right now; we're much too busy.

22. I'll let you **off the hook** about coming to work late if you promise not to do it again.

23. I'm exhausted! I really need a vacation to **get away from it all** for a few days.

24. Wow! Look at Fred's new car. He must be making some **big bucks!**

25. Are you going on vacation again? You must have **money to burn**!

26. Living in a new country **takes some getting used to.**

27. Julia, you **look like a million bucks** in that dress today!

28. I took my new girlfriend to that expensive new restaurant last night. It was great, but it cost me a huge **chunk of change**!

29. I love my new job, but it's a real **headache** getting there through all the city traffic.

30. You have to stop talking to your mother for so long every week. I'm worried that we'll get **slapped with** a huge bill.

# GRAMMAR

*Underline the errors in this conversation. What should the person say?*

**CARRIE:** Hi, Mike. Did you enjoyed your vacation?

**MIKE:** Vacation? It weren't a vacation. Everything possible went wrong.

**CARRIE:** Did it rained?

**MIKE:** Yes, it rained all the time. I spent most of the time drinking coffee in cafés!

**CARRIE:** Did you visited many places?

**MIKE:** No, I didn't went anywhere. It was just too awful to go out. We wasn't happy campers.

**CARRIE:** Well, was it a nice hotel?

**MIKE:** No, it was really old and very expensive.

**CARRIE:** How many money did you paid?

**MIKE:** You don't want to know. Way too much! The only good thing is I spent fewer money than if we was able to go out!

# Emergency 911

## HELP!

If you own a television, you've seen them: amazing **rescues** from burning buildings, **victims** rescued from the bad guys, and lives saved in hospital **ER**s. From the comfort of your couch, you've seen the TV **versions** of real-life drama. The downside of these TV dramas is that they make emergencies seem very simple. Unlike in real life, TV problems are **resolved** in just an hour. But the upside of emergency shows is that people see what they have to do to get help.

The most important information to know in an emergency is a very simple phone number: 911. Even schools teach this number to small children at an early age. There are plenty of stories of kids as young as three years old making a 911 phone call that has saved a life.

The phone number is the same for fire, medical, and police emergencies: 911.

The phone number is the same from both **landlines** and **cell phones**: 911.

When a landline call comes in, the emergency **dispatcher** may be able to see the phone number and the exact **location** of the call, but not always. Calls from a cell phone may not **display** the same information. The most **critical** thing to remember when making an emergency call is to remain calm. It's a **matter of life and death**. You must be understood when making this call. Because everyone tends to speak very quickly and excitedly when they are nervous or afraid, it can be even more difficult to understand second language speakers in an emergency. For this reason, it's **vital** to remember the following instructions:

✓ Stay calm.
✓ Speak slowly and clearly.
✓ Know what information the operator will need.

The **operator** will ask many questions so that she can **get a good picture** of the problem and send exactly the right kind of help. She'll ask for **essential** information like: Who? What? Where? When? It's important to answer all the questions slowly and clearly. Don't worry; she's not wasting time. Even while you're answering her questions, the operator is contacting the right emergency system. You must stay **on the line** with the operator until help arrives. Do not **hang up**!

The 911 dispatchers are specially trained to ask very clear questions about the emergency. The dialogues below are examples of the kinds of conversations you may have. Remember, the operator will ask different questions as he or she learns about your emergency.

## HELP! FIRE!

### DIALOGUE 1: TRACK 28

**DISPATCHER:** 911. What is your emergency?

**CALLER:** HELP!HELP!MYHOUSEMYHOUSE!HURRY!HELPME!

**DISPATCHER:** Ma'am, I can't understand what you're saying. Please calm down. What is your location?

**CALLER:** My house. It's burning! There's a fire in my house! Can you send a fire truck? Help!

**DISPATCHER:** What is the address?

**CALLER:** 123 Peachtree Street! Can you send a fire truck? Please help!

**DISPATCHER:** Help is **on the way**, ma'am. What room is the fire in?

**CALLER:** It's in the kitchen. The curtains **caught fire** when I was cooking. HURRY!

**DISPATCHER:** Are you still in the house?

**CALLER:** Yes! Yes! I'm in the bedroom.

**DISPATCHER:** You must get out of the house right away. Can you do that?

**CALLER:** Yes, the door is right here.

**DISPATCHER:** Ma'am, go outside, but stay on the line with me.

**CALLER:** Okay, okay. I'm outside now. PLEASE HURRY!

**DISPATCHER:** Is there anyone else in the house?

**CALLER:** MY DOG! MY DOG! My dog is in the house!

**DISPATCHER:** Ma'am—Do *NOT* go back into the house. The fire trucks are on the way. The firefighters will find your dog.

**CALLER:** I hear the **sirens**! I can see the truck! They're here! They're here!

 **TIP 1** There is no charge for 911 calls. They are free calls from landlines or cell phones.

 **TIP 2** Mistakes happen. If you dial 911 by mistake, do not just **hang up**. Stay on the phone until the dispatcher answers, and just say, "Sorry, I dialed by mistake." If you just hang up, they may think there is an emergency at your house.

## VOCABULARY

ⓘ **caught fire**: went into flames

• **cell phone**: mobile phone

• **critical** (also **vital, essential**): extremely important

• **dispatcher**: person who sends police or other services where they are needed

• **display**: show

• **ER**: short form for a hospital **E**mergency **R**oom, where emergency victims go

ⓘ **get a good picture**: understand clearly

ⓘ **hang up**: end a phone call after you've called a number

ⓘ **landline**: a home (wired) telephone

• **location**: place

ⓘ **matter of life and death**: a situation of extreme importance

• **on the line**: on the phone; do not hang up

- **on the way**: traveling to the destination
- **operator**: a person who answers phone calls for an agency or company
- **rescue**: save from danger
- **resolved**: settled
- **siren**: the loud noise that goes with the flashing light on the top of an emergency vehicle
- **version**: type, kind
- **victim**: someone who is hurt in some way

## PRONUNCIATION POINTER

The letter groups *augh* and *ough* are very tricky in English. They sound like *aw*. *Caught* sounds like ***cawt***. *Bought* sounds like ***bawt***. *Taught* sounds like ***tawt***.

## GRAMMAR REMINDER 1: Modal Verbs of Necessity: *Have to, Must*

**Have to** shows that something is necessary. **Don't have to** means that something is not necessary. **Have to** can be used in the past, present, or future.
    You **have to** stay calm. (present)
    You**'ll have to** give your address when you call. (future)
    We **had to** call 911. (past)

**Must** also shows that something is necessary. It's stronger than *have to*. You won't hear *must* so much in spoken English, but you'll often see it written. The negative is *must not*, which expresses that something is not allowed. It can be used in the present or future sense only. Its form does not change.
    You **must** stay on the line. (present)
    You **must** call later. (future)
    You **must not** hang up if you call 911 by mistake.

## GRAMMAR REMINDER 2: Modal Verbs for Requests: *Can, Could*

You can use *can* and *could* to ask for something. *Can* may be more common, but *could* is a little more polite.
    **Can** you send a fire truck, please?
    **Could** you send a fire truck, please?

# HELP! HE'S NOT BREATHING!

## DIALOGUE 2: TRACK 29

**OPERATOR:** Paramedic 128. What's the address of your emergency?

**CALLER:** HELP! HELP! I need an ambulance!

**OPERATOR:** Okay, sir, what's the address?

**CALLER:** I'm not sure. I'm outside. It's . . . it's . . . I think it's Taylor Road. It's Lawrenceville. I need an ambulance!

**OPERATOR:** Sir, we'll get help right away. What's the phone number you're calling from?

**CALLER:** Um, it's my cell phone. It's 555-1006. Please hurry. There's a guy here . . . Hurry! Can you send an ambulance?

**OPERATOR:** Okay, sir, what's the **nature** of the emergency?

**CALLER:** There's a guy lying here. He's not **conscious**. He's not breathing! He's not breathing!

**OPERATOR:** Okay. He's not breathing? He's **unconscious**?

**CALLER:** Right.

**OPERATOR:** Okay, sir, an ambulance is on the way. But I need you to start **CPR** right now. I'll help you over the phone until they get there.

**CALLER:** The neighbor is doing CPR, but the guy isn't **responding**. He's not responding! He's not moving and he's not breathing.

**OPERATOR:** Okay, sir, the ambulance is on the way. They'll be there in minutes. Did you **witness** what happened to the man?

**CALLER:** No, I didn't see what happened.

**OPERATOR:** Okay, sir, I've dispatched all this information to the **paramedics**. Keep up the CPR until they get there. They're just a few blocks away.

**CALLER:** Thank you! This guy isn't responding to anything!

**OPERATOR:** Okay they should be there.

**CALLER:** Yeah, here they are! Thank you, sir, thank you.

**OPERATOR:** Okay, sir, call us back if you need any help.

Many public libraries, schools, and hospitals offer free first aid and CPR classes. It's always good to know what to do in an emergency, while you're waiting for help to arrive.

## VOCABULARY

- **CPR**: <u>C</u>ardio <u>P</u>ulmonary <u>R</u>esuscitation; pressing on a person's chest, breathing into his mouth to try to get his heart started again
- **conscious**: awake; aware of surroundings
- **nature**: kind, type
- **paramedics**: specially trained people who can do first aid and some medical treatments in an emergency
- **responding**: reacting
- **unconscious**: not awake; not aware of anything; no reaction of any senses
- **witness**: see

## GRAMMAR REMINDER 3: Modal Verbs of Advice, Possibility, Ability—*Should, Would, Could*

These will all be followed by the verb in its base form.

*Should* is used when giving strong *advice* to do something.
You **should** teach children about emergency calls.

*Would* is used to express what you might do in a certain situation.
I **would** volunteer at the firehouse if I had more time.

*Could* expresses *possibility* and the *ability* to do something in the past.
There **could** be a problem if they don't get enough volunteers.
I **could** run four miles when I was younger.

### PRONUNCIATION POINTER

Another tricky string of letters is *ould*. The letter *l* is not pronounced, so *ould* sounds like **ood**. *Could* sounds like **kood**. *Should* sounds like **shood**. *Would* sounds like **wood**.

## *Grammar Fun Fact!*

Americans sometimes use a funny expression to say that they wish they did something differently. They say, "shoulda woulda coulda." Think things through before you do them, and you'll never have to say, "shoulda woulda coulda"!

## HELP! STRANGER DANGER!

### DIALOGUE 3: TRACK 30

**OPERATOR:** 911. What's the exact location of your emergency?

**CALLER:** Hi, um, well my address is 2495 Cary Street. But it's across the street. I don't know the address.

**OPERATOR:** Okay, ma'am. I didn't get that. Are you on a cell phone? Tell me that address again.

**CALLER:** Yeah, um, it's . . . I don't know, it's 2495 Cary, but it's across the street.

**OPERATOR:** Okay, that's fine. Is that where you're calling me from, ma'am?

**CALLER:** I'm calling you from my cell phone. I think I need the police.

**OPERATOR:** Okay, ma'am. What's the nature of the emergency?

**CALLER:** Well, I'm across the street. I'm not sure . . . My neighbor's away, and, um, um, there are two guys. I think they're **breaking into** the house. Um, it looks like there are two guys. HEY! THEY JUST BROKE A WINDOW! One guy just ripped through the **screen door**! They're looking around to see if anyone saw them! Can you get the police here? Hurry!

**OPERATOR:** Okay, ma'am, we'll have someone there right away. Do you recognize the people at all?

**CALLER:** No, not at all. It's not my neighbor; they're away. **I have no idea** who these guys are, but they just broke the window and **kicked in** the door! I think you need to get the police here fast.

**OPERATOR:** Can you describe the men, ma'am?

**CALLER:** They're inside now. I don't know. I don't know. **To be honest with you**, I didn't really notice what they were wearing or anything. Um, I think one guy was pretty tall. He was wearing some kind of baseball cap, I think. And, uh, the other guy **entered** through the window before I got a good look at him. **All I know is** these guys broke into the house! Can you get the police here?!

**OPERATOR:** Ma'am, they're on their way. Do you know if the guys have a **weapon**?

**CALLER:** I don't know; I couldn't see from my angle. They **had a hard time** trying to kick in the door. Um, but, um, they **smashed** the window with a bat, I think. A baseball bat.

**OPERATOR:** Okay, ma'am, they're on their way. Don't hang up until they get there.

**CALLER:** Okay. Thank you. Wait, okay, here they are! Thank you!

**TIP 4**

If you want to speak with a police officer, but it is *not* an emergency, you should *not* call 911. You can find the phone number of the local **precinct** in your phone book.

## VOCABULARY

- **all I know is**: a strong way to say *this is the important fact*
- **breaking in**: forcing one's way in
- **entered**: went in
- ⓘ **had a hard time**: had difficulty with something
- ⓘ **I have no idea**: a stronger way to say *I don't know*
- ⓘ **kick in**: hit with one's foot and smash open
- **precinct**: local police station
- **screen door**: an outer door that allows air into the room, but not the bugs!
- ⓘ **smashed**: broke suddenly and noisily
- ⓘ **to be honest with you**: a way of saying *really*
- **weapon**: something that is used to hurt someone

## MORE FUN WITH IDIOMATIC EXPRESSIONS: Fire

- **You're fired!**: bad-news words for when you lose your job
  *You've been late every day for the last two weeks, and you haven't finished one project. **You're fired!***

- **Holy smokes!:** Wow!
  *Holy smokes, my neighbor just won a thousand dollars!*

- **old flame:** a former boyfriend or girlfriend
*Susan was not happy when her boyfriend kept talking about his **old flame**.*

- **out of the frying pan and into the fire**: going from a bad situation to a worse one
*She thought it was a bad day when the bus splashed her new skirt, but it was **out of the frying pan and into the fire** when she spilled hot coffee and burned herself.*

- **fire off**: write something quickly and send it off immediately
*When she read the article in the newspaper about the animal shelter, she wanted to **fire off** an e-mail to her friends to ask them to help.*

| | |
|---|---|
|  **Did You Spot It?** | Remember: *could* is also used for ability in the past. In this example, *couldn't* means *was not able to* see. **Example:** I **couldn't** see from my angle. |

# What's Up, Doc?

Road to Recovery

## Under the Weather

Aaah-choo! Oh, boy, that **stuffy nose** you've had all week is getting worse. You're **sneezing**, you have a headache, you're **achy** all over, and your throat is **sore**. These **symptoms** can mean only one thing: time to head to the doctor. But who? For most common problems like colds and flu, a **general practitioner** should be your first choice. These doctors are also called *family doctors* because they treat **patients** of all ages, and they take care of most common illnesses. For some more serious problems, the **GP** may suggest that you see a specialist. The GP will be able to make a **recommendation**, and she will provide a **referral** if your health insurance plan requires one.

But if you're new in the neighborhood, you may not know what general practitioner to call. Sometimes the best way to find a doctor is to ask someone you trust. Ask a neighbor or a friend at work. Your **employer** will help you find a list of doctors who participate in your **health plan**.

## DIALOGUE 1: TRACK 31

**ALAN:** Hi, Lia. I haven't seen you for a few days. Where have you been?

**LIA:** I haven't been hiding. I haven't been feeling well for a couple of days, so I've been trying to get lots of rest. I don't think it's working because I still feel sick.

**ALAN:** Wow, maybe you should get **checked out** by a doctor.

**LIA:** I think so, too, but I don't have a family doctor yet. Can you recommend someone?

**ALAN:** We love our GP. She's very patient, and she'll answer every question you ask. She doesn't **rush** you. You should call for an appointment. In fact, if you're really sick, she'll **squeeze you in** right away, even without an appointment.

**LIA:** But what if it's not a cold? What if it's serious? What if I need to see a specialist? What if I need a hospital?

**ALAN:** Calm down. It's probably just the **flu**. Call Dr. Patelli. I'm sure you'll feel better after you talk to her.

**TIP 1** Many doctors have this sign at the **reception desk**: "Payment must be made at time of service." If you can't pay, the doctor will help you with a payment plan.

**TIP 2** Bring something to read! Sometimes there is a long wait at the doctor's office. There are usually magazines in the office, but they could be old or boring. Plus, sick people have been touching them!

## VOCABULARY

- **achy** (also **ache**): a dull body pain (an *achy* feeling is different from a *sharp pain*)
- ⓘ **checked out**: examined, looked at
- **employer:** the person or company you work for; the boss
- **flu:** an illness that makes you sneezy and just feel really bad and achy all over
- **general practitioner**: a type of doctor who sees people with the most common illnesses
- **GP**: short name for a *General Practitioner*

- **health plan**: an insurance benefit provided by some employers for employees (and sometimes their family members) who become ill
- **patient**: someone who is receiving health care
- **reception desk**: the counter or window where you sign in to see the doctor
- **recommendation**: a suggestion
- **referral**: a doctor's recommendation of another doctor
- **rush**: hurry
- **sneezing**: aaah-choo!
- **sore**: hurting
- ⓘ **squeeze someone in**: make time to see someone, even if they don't have an appointment
- ⓘ **stuffy nose**: a feeling that you can't take in air through your nose
- **symptoms**: signs of illness

## Health Insurance: What's Up with That?

Although every country tries to find the best way to provide health care for its citizens, it seems there is no one system that is perfect for everyone. In the United States, **health insurance** is a huge issue. How can we be sure everyone has **access** to excellent health care? How can we help people pay for doctors and expensive **treatments**? What will a family do if someone becomes seriously **ill** and needs **hospitalization**? Medical care in the United States can be very expensive, and no one wants people to suffer because they can't pay.

Most large companies and some small businesses offer health insurance **benefits** to their **employees**. This means that they participate in a health insurance plan and **cover** some of the costs. Other costs for the plan will be **deducted** from the employee's paycheck. This is usually the best option for employees, but there are many plans and many rules, so it's important to get all the information from the **human resources department** at your job or from your employer. A very important thing to remember is that, if you have health insurance through your job, you usually must use a doctor in the insurance **network**. Many insurance companies have arrangements with certain doctors to charge only a certain amount for care. In most cases, your insurance will only pay for doctors in the network. If you choose a doctor who is not in the plan, you will have to pay most of the costs for service yourself.

Many health insurance plans say that you must choose a **primary care physician**. This is the doctor that you will see first whenever you have a problem. If the doctor feels that you need more **specialized** care, the health insurer may require a referral to the specialist. This isn't as complicated as it sounds. Most doctors are very **knowledgeable** about insurance rules. Doctors often have a **staff member** whose only job is to **deal with** the insurance companies.

Once you see the doctor, it's possible that she may **prescribe** a **medication** for your **condition**. She will write the name of the medicine and the **dose** on a special form. Take the **prescription** to the drugstore. The **pharmacist** will ask for your insurance card and fill the prescription. He may **substitute** a **generic drug** unless your physician **specifically** requests a **name brand**. If you have prescription coverage in your health plan, you'll only need to pay a **co-pay**. The insurance will pay the rest of the cost. Insurance plans are complicated, but it's worth taking time to figure them out!

## DIALOGUE 2: TRACK 32

**LIA:** Hi. My name is Lia. I called a **little while** ago. My neighbor recommended that I come in to see Dr. Patelli.

**RECEPTIONIST:** Yes, of course. First, I'll need you to fill out this form with your **health history**. It's for your **chart**. While you're doing that, I'll make a copy of your insurance information.

**LIA:** Oh, no! I didn't bring any information with me! What do you need? Do I need to call my job?

**RECEPTIONIST:** No, it's okay. You don't have to call them now. But didn't you get an insurance card with your **group number**?

**LIA:** Oh! I think I have a little card that has my name and a bunch of numbers on it. Is that what you mean?

**RECEPTIONIST:** Exactly! That's all the information I need. We'll process all the **insurance claims** for you if we have those numbers.

**LIA:** Whew! I think worrying about this insurance was making me sicker than my illness! Will it take a long time for me to see the doctor?

**RECEPTIONIST:** Well, we know patients sometimes have to wait a long time for lots of doctors. Dr. Patelli tries to be respectful of her patients. She won't make you wait unless there's an emergency and she has to squeeze someone in. The nurse will take you in and take your **vital signs**, and then Dr. Patelli will come in to examine you. After she makes her **diagnosis**, she'll write a prescription if you need one. But she will always leave time for you to ask questions. She wants you to understand exactly why she thinks a certain medicine will help.

**LIA:** I think I like this doctor already!

**TIP 3**

Once you've received your prescription, you can drop it off at the drive-thru and pick up the medicine later. Yes, many pharmacies have a drive-thru. But you won't be getting a cheeseburger at *this* drive-thru!

**TIP 4**

Hundreds of specialists deal with only one kind of problem. Here is a list of some of them:

- **cardiologist**: heart problems
- **dermatologist**: skin problems
- **OB/GYN (obstetrician/gynecologist)**: pregnancy, childbirth, and women's health-care issues
- **oncologist**: cancer treatment
- **orthopedist**: bone-related problems
- **pediatrician**: children's illnesses
- **plastic surgeon** (also called a **cosmetic surgeon**): improving the appearance of the body
- **psychiatrist**: mental concerns or illnesses

# VOCABULARY

- **access**: ability to use
- **benefits**: something special the employer offers
- **chart**: your health record and diagnosis
- **condition**: illness
- **co-pay**: the amount you must pay before the insurance company pays the rest of the cost
- **cover**: pay for
- ⓘ **deal with**: handle all the communication with
- **deducted**: taken out of
- **diagnosis**: the decision about what your illness is

- **dose**: the amount of medicine you must take and how often you take it
- **employee**: the worker
- **generic drug**: medicine that has the same formula as a name-brand drug, but it is made at a smaller company
- **group number**: identification of your company so the insurance company knows exactly what to pay
- **health history**: a list of any illnesses you've had in the past, which helps the doctor understand your problem
- **health insurance**: a plan that will pay for your medical bills
- **hospitalization**: being placed into a hospital for treatment
- **human resources department** (also called **personnel**): the department that deals with the workers
- **ill**: sick
- **insurance claim**: a form that tells the insurance company what your illness is and how much they should pay the doctor for your costs
- **knowledgeable**: knowing a lot about something
- **little while**: a short amount of time
- **medication** (also called **medicine** or **drug**): something that will help you get well
- **name brand**: made by a well-known company
- **network**: a group
- **pharmacist**: specially trained professional who will prepare your medicine according to the doctor's prescription
- **prescribe**: write a note for a medicine
- **prescription**: a special form with your name and the dose of the medicine you must take
- **primary care physician**: the doctor, usually a GP, whom you will see first for any illness
- **specialized**: dealing with only one kind of problem
- **specifically**: specially
- **staff member**: office worker
- **substitute**: use to take the place of
- **treatment**: care
- **vital signs**: usually your height, weight, blood pressure, and heart rate (These are usually checked at each visit.)

## GRAMMAR REMINDER: Modals Review

Here are those modals again! See how useful they are?

Check in this unit for all of these examples:
- **should** for giving advice
- **must** to show a strong obligation
- **could** for possibility

## Fun Fact!

English has lots of health-based sayings. Here are two common ones:
- Early to bed, early to rise, makes a man healthy, wealthy, and wise.
- An apple a day keeps the doctor away.

So, eat lots of apples and get lots of sleep. Just don't eat the apples while you sleep!

## MORE FUN WITH IDIOMATIC EXPRESSIONS: Health

- **be/feel under the weather:** feel a little sick
  *He woke up with a sneeze and **felt under the weather**.*

- **take a turn for the worse:** have an illness that gets more serious
  *Later that day, he **took a turn for the worse**, so he called the doctor.*

- **in bad shape:** in very bad health
  *The doctor said that he was **in such bad shape** that he should go straight to bed.*

- **clean bill of health:** information that one's health is excellent
  *He took some medicine and got lots of rest. After a few days, the doctor gave him a **clean bill of health**.*

- **the picture of health:** in excellent health
  *Now he looks well rested and **the picture of health**.*

# What's Up Now?

**Good Health**

## Open Wide

Eeew! The dentist! No one likes going to the dentist in any language! We don't want to **offend** dentists out there, but we **bet** even dentists don't like going to the dentist. Still, it's one of those things that must be done. Most dentists recommend a **checkup** every six months. The **hygienist** will do a **cleaning**, and the dentist will check for any problems and make sure the mouth looks healthy. But you know it's bad news when you wake up with a **throbbing** headache and a pain in your mouth. What a nightmare! There's no time to wait for your regular checkup appointment; you need to **have it checked out** immediately. **Oh, come on**; it's not so bad. Don't think of it as 20 minutes you're spending with your mouth wide open, while someone puts sharp **instruments** in it and **pokes** around. Think of it this way: you're spending 20 minutes in a big **comfy** chair while someone else is home taking care of the kids! (Somehow, we think you're *not* **buying** that . . .)

## DIALOGUE 1: TRACK 33

**DR. SMILEY:** Hi, Lia. What seems to be the problem today?

**LIA:** I hope you can tell me! A **chunk** of my tooth broke off yesterday.

**DR. SMILEY:** That's not good. Did you bite something hard?

**LIA:** No, I didn't . . . that's the **weird** thing. It just kind of fell out.

**DR. SMILEY:** Did it hurt when it broke?

**LIA:** Yes, it did, just a little; but it started to hurt **like crazy** this morning.

**DR. SMILEY:** I think **we'd better** take a full set of X-rays . . . Okay, **open wide**. Let me take a look. Oh, boy. Yes, it looks like you've **exposed** the **root** on your left **molar**.

**LIA:** *rgscht rfghsh!! ghs gtfhhkj?*

**DR. SMILEY:** Sorry. I'll be done in a minute. **I'm afraid** you'll have to have a **root canal**. I can put in a **temporary filling**, but you'll have to come back in two weeks for the **procedure**.

**LIA:** Do I *have to* have a root canal? My tooth doesn't really hurt too much.

**DR. SMILEY:** If we don't take care of this quickly, it may become **infected**, and it will hurt a lot. I'll tell Dina to set up an appointment, and I'll see you back here **in** two weeks, **on** Tuesday, the 14th, at 3 p.m.

**LIA:** Will the procedure hurt?

**DR. SMILEY:** I'll give you **medication** so that you won't feel any pain. Relax! It's not so bad!

 **TIP 1** Regular visits to the dentist can prevent problems from happening. The dentist is your friend! Yes, really!

## VOCABULARY

- ⓘ **bet**: be pretty sure
- • **checkup**: an examination to be sure everything is healthy
- ⓘ **chunk**: a big piece
- • **cleaning**: removing anything that is on the teeth
- ⓘ **comfy**: comfortable
- • **exposed**: open

- **filling**: substance put into a hole in the tooth to protect it
- ⓘ **freebie**: something special you get without paying
- ⓘ **have something checked out**: have something looked at or examined
- **hygienist**: professional who cleans your teeth with special tools
- ⓘ **I'm afraid**: unfortunately
- **infected**: filled with bacteria and very sore!
- **instruments**: special tools
- ⓘ **like crazy**: A LOT!
- **medication**: medicine
- **molar**: large tooth in the back of the mouth
- ⓘ **not buying**: not believing
- **offend**: cause someone to feel angry or upset
- ⓘ **oh, come on**: *really!*
- ⓘ **open wide**: open your mouth (so I can get these dental tools in there and find the problem!)
- **poke**: touch, in a sharp way
- **procedure**: process of repairing something
- **root**: the base part of the tooth, under the gums (mouth tissue)
- **root canal**: dental procedure removing material around the root of the tooth
- **temporary**: for a short time
- **throbbing**: aching, almost vibrating
- ⓘ **we'd better**: we should
- **weird**: strange

## *Fun Fact!*

At your regular dental checkups, the hygienist will usually give you some **freebies**: a new toothbrush, some floss, and maybe some new products to try. Maybe they just want you to keep coming back . . .

## GRAMMAR REMINDER 1: The Past Simple Tense—
## Short Answers

For short answers to past simple questions, *don't* repeat the verb. Simply say: **Yes, I did** or **No, I didn't**. We usually use the contraction in short answers.

*Examples:*
Did you bite something hard? *No, I didn't.*
Did it hurt when it broke? *Yes, it did.*

**Remember:** The answer will be different with that wacky verb *to be*!
**Examples:**
Were you eating something hard? *Yes, I was.*
Was it very painful at the time? *No, it wasn't!*

## GRAMMAR REMINDER 2: Prepositions of Time
Use the prepositions *in, at*, or *on* to talk about time.
**Examples:**
*In* is used for periods of time.
*in two weeks; in three months; in ten years*

*At* is used for an exact time.
*at 3 p.m.; at noon*

*On* is used for days and dates.
*on Tuesday; on August 6*

## MORE FUN WITH IDIOMATIC EXPRESSIONS: Teeth

- **sink your teeth into something**: do something in an excited way
  *This is a well-written book about an interesting subject. I can really **sink my teeth into it.***

- **lie through your teeth**: lie about something everyone knows is false
  *He was soaking wet, so he was **lying through his teeth** when he said he had not gone into the lake.*

- **by the skin of your teeth**: just barely manage to escape a big problem
  *Wow, that was close! I missed crashing my bike into that car **by the skin of my teeth.***

- **like pulling teeth**: do something with a lot of difficulty
  *It was **like pulling teeth** when the woman tried to get her cell phone company to discuss a cheaper rate.*

- **bite off more than you can chew**: take on more work than you can handle at the time
  *She **bit off more than she could chew** when she agreed to work extra hours on the busy holiday weekend.*

# Let's See . . .

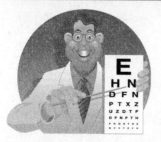

See here. A regular visit to the eye doctor is another important step in keeping healthy, but when it comes to taking care of your vision, things can become a little **fuzzy**. Not all eye care is covered by health insurance. Many health plans will not pay for glasses, but most will cover medical care of eye diseases. Three kinds of professionals specialize in care of the eyes: **opticians, optometrists,** and **ophthalmologists.**

An optician is a professional who makes the glasses that an optometrist or ophthalmologist prescribes for a patient.

An optometrist can examine the eyes and prescribe corrective lenses. He can also treat some eye problems. An optometrist is not an **M.D.**, but he has completed **pre-med** courses at a university and graduate courses at a college of optometry.

For serious eye problems, you should see an ophthalmologist, an eye professional who is an M.D. and who can perform surgery on the eye if necessary.

## DIALOGUE 2: TRACK 34

**LIA:** Hi. I'm here for my eye examination. I know I'm a little early. My appointment is at 2 p.m.

**DR. SPECS:** That's fine. Is this your regular checkup, or have you been having any problems?

**LIA:** Well, I'm about **due** for my checkup, but I'm a little **concerned** about some headaches I've been having lately.

**DR. SPECS:** Hmm. Have you been under any extra **stress** at work or at home lately? That could cause some of your symptoms.

**LIA:** I'm *always* under stress! But maybe that's all it is.

**DR. SPECS:** Let's just check things out to be sure there's no **underlying** problem. How about your family history? Any eye problems that you know of?

**LIA:** Actually, my grandmother had **glaucoma**, and my dad takes drops to control his eye pressure. Oh, yeah, and my mom had **cataracts** removed.

**DR. SPECS:** Well, I think it's important to do a **thorough** exam. I'm going to check your vision, look at both the inside and outside of your eyes, and measure the **pressure**. I'll need to **dilate** your **pupils,** so it'll be a little while before you can drive home. And we'll check the prescription for your glasses.

**LIA:** I'll feel much better to know everything's okay. Now that you mention it, maybe my prescription needs to be changed. Could that be causing my headaches?

**DR. SPECS:** Sure it could. We'll check it out. If everything's okay, I'll see you back in two years for a regular checkup.

**TIP 2**

If you need to get glasses, there are plenty of places to get the prescription filled. But remember, you also can find anything on the Internet! There are websites that will take your prescription and send you exactly the cool **frames** you want—usually at a much lower price than the stores in your local mall. Yay! We love a bargain!

## VOCABULARY

- **cataracts**: cloudy spots on the clear layers of the eye
- **concerned**: worried
- **dilate**: make the pupil of the eye open wider
- **due**: expected
- **frames**: the metal or plastic part of eyeglasses (that can make you look like a rock star!)
- **fuzzy**: blurry; not clear
- **glaucoma**: a disease of the eye that causes high pressure inside the eye
- **M.D.**: Medical Doctor, or physician, who has completed medical school and hospital training
- **pressure**: the force of something pressing
- **pre-med**: courses leading to a medical doctor's degree
- **pupil**: the small black opening in the center of the eye
- **stress**: tension caused by worrying
- **thorough**: complete
- **underlying**: below; not easily seen

## MORE FUN WITH IDIOMATIC EXPRESSIONS: Eyes

- **a sight for sore eyes**: something that is wonderful to see
  *Lin hadn't seen James for months. When he came home, he was a **sight for sore eyes**.*

- **in the public eye**: able to be seen by many people
  *When the newspaper wrote about the politician's mistake, he was not happy to be **in the public eye**.*

- **look someone straight in the eye**: look at someone without shame or embarrassment
  *After the waiter spilled the woman's soup, he was so embarrassed that he couldn't **look her straight in the eye**.*

- **not see eye to eye**: disagree
  *They couldn't **see eye to eye** on their vacation plans. He wanted to go to the beach, and she wanted to go to the mountains.*

- **turn a blind eye**: pretend not to see something
  *He wasn't supposed to have cookies before lunch, but his grandmother **turned a blind eye** when she saw him reach for the box.*

### *Fun Fact!*

You can't sneeze with your eyes open! It's impossible. (Try it, if you don't believe us.)

## WOOF!

Are you a pet lover? Do you share your home with a **furry** little friend who **wags** his **tail** when you come home from work, or who jumps in your lap and **purrs**? Do you share your **ice cream cone** with little Rover? Is he **snuggled** in your comfy chair? Pet lovers will tell you that their little friend is like **one of the family** . . . Woof! That means that little Rover gets lots of **TLC** . . . just like the kids! The upside of pet ownership is that no matter how bad a day you have, little Rover will be excited to see you. The downside is that you are **committed** to taking care of one more **creature** with aches and pains. In the United States, a doctor who is specially trained to treat animals is called a **veterinarian**. What's the matter? Can't say that one fast? Ha! Neither can most Americans! Because it's such a **tongue twister**, most people refer to an animal doctor as "the vet." We can all say that one!

## DIALOGUE 3: TRACK 35

**VET:** I haven't seen little Rover here for quite a while. What seems to be the problem?

**LIA:** I'm really worried about him. You know he's always been a very active dog, but lately he seems to be very **stiff** in the back legs. If he's been lying down for a while, he has a tough time getting up. When he walks, I've noticed that he **limps.**

**VET:** Has he had any type of **injury**?

**LIA:** No, just the usual running and jumping. Nothing else.

**VET:** I know he's a pretty active dog, but **hip** problems are quite common in that **breed.** Let me check him out thoroughly. I think we'll need to get some X-rays to **see what's going on** here. I'll have to **sedate** him before doing the tests. Is that okay?

**LIA:** Sure, do anything you have to do. Can you do the tests now?

**VET:** No, you'll have to bring him in tomorrow. It will take a little while for the **sedative** to work, and then he'll need some time to wake up from it.

**LIA:** My poor little Rover!

**VET:** Let's plan on tomorrow morning, **first thing.** Is that OK for you?

**LIA: Absolutely!** I'll have him here first thing. What time do you open?

**TIP 3**

Health insurance is such a great idea for people that someone **figured out** it would be just as good for people's pets. Yes, you can buy health insurance for Rover! Your vet will have all the **details**. That's de—TAILS. Haha!

## VOCABULARY

ⓘ **absolutely!**: for sure! of course!
* **breed**: type, kind
* **committed**: decided to do something
* **creature**: animal
* **details**: all items of information
ⓘ **figured out**: had an idea; understood
* **first thing**: as early as possible

- **furry**: covered in fur
- **hip**: the bone joint between the waist and the legs
- **ice cream cone**: a serving of ice cream in a cone-shaped cookie
- **injury**: hurt caused by some event
- **limps**: walks with difficulty because of a hurt leg
- ⓘ **one of the family**: as if an actual member of the human family
- **purrs**: makes a vibrating sound (that's a happy cat!)
- **sedate**:make calm, tranquil with medicine
- **sedative**: a medicine that puts you to sleep
- ⓘ **see what's going on**: see what the situation is
- **snuggled**: sitting comfortably
- **stiff**: hard to move
- **tail**: the back part of an animal (it's what the dog wags!)
- **TLC**: Tender, Loving Care; what we give to those we love
- **tongue twister**: a word or expression that is very difficult to say
- **veterinarian**: animal doctor
- **wags**: moves from side to side in an excited way
- **wealthy**: rich; having lots of money
- **will**: an official paper that explains what must be done with your money after your death

### Fun Fact!
A very **wealthy** woman in New York City left $12 MILLION in her **will** for her little dog. Woof, woof!

**TIP 4**

Make friends with the doggie next door. You never know if he'll be a millionaire one day. Haha!

## MORE FUN WITH IDIOMATIC EXPRESSIONS: Dogs

- **as sick as a dog**: very sick
  *I missed the party because I **was as sick as a dog**; I just stayed in bed.*

- **fight like cats and dogs**: fight or argue a lot
  *They're best friends now, but when they were young kids, it seemed that they always **fought like cats and dogs.***

- **raining cats and dogs**: raining very hard
  *The hurricane left the area, but it was still **raining cats and dogs**.*

- **you can't teach an old dog new tricks**: it's very hard for someone to change the way they do things
  *Margaret tried to teach her grandmother how to use e-mail, but her grandmother just couldn't figure out the computer. Grandma just said, "I'd rather just write a letter on paper. **You can't teach an old dog new tricks.**"*

- **going to the dogs**: getting bad
  *His lunch business started **going to the dogs** when the stores next to him closed.*

# Review: Units 10–12

## VOCABULARY

*Fill in the missing words. The first letter is there to help you.*

1. Did you hear about poor Jenny? She was the v_____ of a burglary yesterday. Someone broke into her house and stole all her money and jewelry.

2. I had a bad car accident last week. I was knocked u _____, so I don't remember anything, but I feel fine now.

3. Paul was a w_____ when the bus bumped into the parked car. When the police arrived to help, Paul was able to give helpful information about what happened.

4. I think I have the flu. I have all the s_____: headache, sneezing, and runny nose. I think I'll go up to bed.

5. If you are going to s_____, it's best to use a tissue so you don't spread any germs.

6. My body a_____s all over after running 10 miles yesterday.

7. When you go to the doctor, make sure you're prepared to pay your c_____.

8. I was so tired this morning that the guy behind me had to p_____ me when the bus line started to move.

9. I really don't want to go to the dentist today. My tooth hurts a lot, so she's going to do a r_____ c_____ procedure.

10. I'll need someone to pick me up from the eye doctor today. He's going to d_____ my pupils, so I won't be able to drive.

## INFORMAL LANGUAGE

*Fill in the blanks in the idiomatic expressions. Can you explain what they mean?*

11. I thought the new job would be better than the old one, but actually it was out of the _____ pan and into the fire.

12. Poor Aunt Hilda is in bad _____ after falling and breaking her arm. I should go and visit her tomorrow.

13. You look like the _____ of health after your vacation in the Caribbean!

14. I love getting new projects at work, especially interesting ones that I can really _____ my teeth into.

15. He was so lucky to survive the accident. He escaped by the _____ of his teeth.

16. It's wonderful to see you after such a long time. You're a(n) _____ for sore eyes!

17. The mother turned a(n) _____ eye when her son pretended he was doing his homework while he played on the computer.

18. Poor Tony. After he ate that huge Thanksgiving meal, he was as sick as a(n) _____.

19. It's no good. I just don't understand these computers. I guess you just can't teach an old dog new _____!

20. The neighbor's kids are so noisy. They fight like _____ and dogs all the time.

## GRAMMAR

*Choose the correct modal verbs for the sentences. Can you explain why you need that one?*

21. If there's a fire, you (*can/have to*) get out of the building as quickly as possible.

22. The doctor says I (*should/would*) stop smoking if I want to be healthy.

23. (*Could/should*) you open the window, please? It's really hot in here!

24. You (*should/can*) always wear sunscreen on sunny days to protect your skin.

25. I love having a day off because I (*don't have to/wouldn't* ) get up early.

26. You'll (*have to/had*) stay at home tomorrow if you still feel sick.

27. We (*should/had to*) call 911 last week when our house caught fire.

28. I (*can/could*) run 10 miles a day when I was younger.

29. I (*should/would*) buy a new car if I had more money.

30. You (*would/could*) have an accident if you keep driving this fast.

# Around Town

Town Center

## Where Am I?

**Settling in** feels great, doesn't it? There's a comfortable feeling of being **at home**, and a big part of the fun is just to **scope out** the neighborhood. There are plenty of fun places to discover, but it's great to know that there are lots of places nearby that can help you with just about anything you may need. Maybe you're thinking, "The first thing I need to do is **write home**." We agree! You **miss** family and friends, and they miss you. (Well, we hope they do.) It's time for a long letter with the latest **scoop** and all the **gossip** about your new life in the United States. Hmm. But how does the letter get from your table to the table far away in your home country?

The U.S. Post Office can get the job done! Mail is **reliable** in the United States, and it's inexpensive and convenient. There's a **central location** in most **apartment complexes** for individual mailboxes. The postal worker will put the letters in your box and leave **parcels** in a safe place. You can **pick up** your mail here, and there's a place to leave mail that's going out. In some neighborhoods, there's a special large metal container where you can **drop** off mail. **Pickups** of that mail are scheduled at regular times during the day.

If you live in a house, you probably have your own mailbox next to the street. You can leave your outgoing mail there, but be sure to put up the little flag. That's the **signal** to the mail carrier that there's something to collect. In a larger city, there will just be a **slot** in your front door. The mailman will put your mail into the slot. Let's hope your little dog friend, Rover, doesn't think it's lunch!

Be sure to have the proper **postage** on the envelope, or the post office will return it to you, marked "Return to Sender. **Insufficient** Postage." (Don't forget to include a **return address** on the envelope.) If you don't have **stamps,** or if you want to mail a package, you'll need to head to the post office. The worker will weigh your parcel and give you several mailing choices. Regular mail is pretty **speedy** in the United States, but you may want to be *sure* that something will arrive quickly. You can choose **Priority Mail,** which usually arrives within the United States in three to four days. **Express Mail** will get your letter or package to a U.S. recipient the very next day, but this can be pretty expensive. You'll be able to choose to **insure** the mail and to get notices about its delivery.

While you're out on the post office errand, plan to stop at the local library. It's not just about books, although you can find anything at all that you want to read. It doesn't cost anything to get a library card, and you'll be able to **check out** as many books as you want for free. You'll need to return the books by the **due date,** or you'll pay a small fine. This fine increases every day the book is late, so it can **add up** pretty quickly. If you want a book that isn't **checked in**, you can **reserve** a copy, and the **librarian** will notify you when it comes in. By the way, you can also just relax with the newspaper and a cup of coffee; many libraries have small cafés. And check out the DVDs, videos, music CDs, and **audiobooks**, so you have plenty to listen to on those long **commutes!** You'll be **amazed** at the cool things happening at the library. There are classes for just about any interest you may have: managing your money, knitting, learning computer skills, and starting art projects. Of course, there are book discussion groups for all types of books and **Story Hours** for the kids. And most libraries in most towns offer English classes for practice and conversation. These classes are almost always free. Cool!

Don't forget your local **town hall** or **municipal building** as another great resource for information. At the municipal building, you can view everything from airplane **flight plans** that might affect your neighborhood to property limits and **zoning requirements**. You can learn about any town **ordinances** you may need to know. If you want to **put up** a fence or build a **deck**, you'll need to get a **permit**. There are rules and **building codes** about where you can put **additions** and rules about how big they can be. You'll have to pay for a permit, but it's better than paying a **stiff** fine for not getting one!

## DIALOGUE 1: TRACK 36

**ALAN:** Hey, Lia, that's a pretty big parcel you have. Can I **give you a hand**? Where are you going?

**LIA:** Thanks, Alan. Actually, it's not that heavy, just a little **bulky**. I'm sending some American jeans home to my sister, so I'm headed to the post office. I thought it was on this block. Can you tell me where it is?

**ALAN:** Oh, it's not far. It's right around the block. Go to that **corner** and **make a right**. When you get to the **crosswalk**, cross the street. You'll see the post office in the middle of the next block. **You can't miss it;** you'll see the **Stars and Stripes** hanging over the entrance.

**LIA:** Hey, thanks. By the way, where are *you* headed? If you're not busy, would you like to **grab a quick bite** somewhere?

**ALAN:** Great idea! I'm **on my way** to the library, and there's a nice café in the **lobby**. We could have a quick bite or some coffee and then see what new magazines have arrived. They usually put the new ones on the table near the sofa. I also want to find out about the new English conversation class that's starting this week. It meets **once** a week, and I **figure** it's a great way to meet new friends while I practice English.

**LIA:** English classes? This week? **Count me in**! I didn't know the library was in this neighborhood. How do we get there?

**ALAN:** It's just two blocks from the post office, between the bank and the drugstore. We cross the avenue and then turn left. That's about a five-minute walk from here.

**LIA:** Let's go!

If you have a skill or **hobby**, your library wants you! Local libraries offer lots of classes, and they are always happy to find volunteers who will teach their hobbies to others.

Be sure to find out if you need a license to own a pet in your town. Sometimes there is a limit on how many dogs or cats you can have. There are also noise ordinances, so if your pets (or your parties!) make a lot of noise after a certain time, you may get a visit from the **code enforcement** people.

# VOCABULARY

- **add up**: get more expensive
- **additions**: structures that you add to your house
- **amazed**: very surprised
- **apartment complexes**: groups of apartment buildings
- ⓘ **at home**: feeling comfortable, as if at home
- ⓘ **audiobooks**: books you can listen to
- **building code**: rules about how something may be built, for example, materials and size
- **bulky**: big and a little hard to manage, but not necessarily heavy in weight
- **central location**: a place convenient to most people
- **checked in**: available on the shelf
- **check out**: sign out a book or other material with your library card
- **code enforcement** person: someone from the town whose job is to handle complaints about anyone not following the town ordinances
- **commute**: trip to work
- **corner**: where two blocks meet
- ⓘ **count me in**: I want to be included!
- **crosswalk**: a specially marked area to cross the street at a corner
- **deck**: an open structure outside a house
- ⓘ **drop off**: leave something or someone at a place
- **due date**: when you must bring the book back
- ⓘ **figure**: believe; think
- **flight plans**: if an airport schedules planes to fly over your neighborhood
- ⓘ **give someone a hand**: help someone
- **gossip**: exciting or surprising information, often about other people
- ⓘ **grab a quick bite**: have a quick, casual small meal or snack
- **hobby**: something that you like to do in your free time
- **insufficient**: not enough
- **insure**: pay for a service that will pay you for the package if it is lost
- **librarian**: the library worker
- **lobby**: large open area before the main room
- ⓘ **make a right**: turn right
- **miss**: feel sad to be without someone or something

- **municipal building** (also called **town hall**): building where the town or city offices are
- **once**: one time
- ⓘ **on my way**: headed for, going to
- **ordinances**: rules about noise and pets in a neighborhood
- **parcel**: package
- **permit**: a document allowing you to build something
- ⓘ **pick up** (verb; two words): collect; gather
- **pickup**: (noun; one word): process of collecting something
- **postage**: the stamps needed to mail something
- **Priority Mail, Express Mail**: two fast delivery options that cost extra
- ⓘ **put up**: build
- **reliable**: efficient; dependable
- **reserve**: have the library save the book for you when it comes in
- **return address**: your name and address, which you put in the upper left corner of the envelope
- ⓘ **scoop**: information
- ⓘ **scope out**: explore; find out about things
- **settling in** (also **settling down**): getting used to your new place; getting comfortable
- **signal**: a sign
- **slot**: a small opening, usually in machines, that will accept a letter or a coin
- **speedy**: fast
- **stamps**: postage in different denominations
- **Stars and Stripes**: an informal name for the American flag (Can you guess why?)
- ⓘ **stiff**: harsh, extreme
- **Story Hour**: a time (usually at a library) when children may come to hear a story read to them
- **write home**: send a letter home
- ⓘ **you can't miss it**: it's obvious, very clear to see
- **zoning requirements**: rules about what you can build on your property

*Library* is a tricky word to pronounce. It sure seems like there are a lot of r's in that word, and we should hear them both! The word sounds like *lie-brerry*.

### Fun Fact!
In the *Batman* comic books, Batgirl was a librarian. We bet she didn't have to tell the kids to *shhhh!* more than once.

## MORE FUN WITH IDIOMATIC EXPRESSIONS:
### Prepositions of Place

**up in the air:** uncertain; not sure
*Her plans to go to the movies were **up in the air** until she knew if she had to work late.*

**under the weather:** feeling sick
*Doctors say you should stay home from work if you're feeling **under the weather**. Don't make others sick!*

**over my head:** too complicated to understand
*I couldn't understand their conversation about the mathematics of space and the planets; it was way **over my head**.*

**around the corner:** happening soon
*Wow, the summer was just ending, but the decorations in the store made her feel that Halloween was just **around the corner**.*

**out of the loop:** not knowing what's going on
*Mary Ellen's entire family was planning a vacation, but Mary Ellen was so busy with her work project that she felt completely **out of the loop**.*

## GRAMMAR REMINDER 1: Prepositions of Place

*On, around, in, over, near,* and *between* are all prepositions of place. They indicate *where* something is. Did you spot them in the dialogue?

*on* this block
*around* the block
*in* the middle of the next block
*over* the entrance
*on* the table
*near* the sofa
*in* this neighborhood
*between* the bank and the drugstore

## GRAMMAR REMINDER 2: The Present Continuous Tense—Affirmative Statements

The present continuous is used to talk about things happening at this moment. Use the verb *to be* and the *ing* form of the verb. We usually use the contractions, especially when speaking.

I **am** send**ing**. (I'm sending.)
You **are** send**ing**. (You're sending.)

**Note:** Don't be confused! Some books call this tense the *present continuous,* and some call it the *present progressive.* It's the same tense!

## At Your Service

There are **tons** of **services** available in every city and town to help you with any need. Sometimes it can be **confusing** to know how to find what you're looking for. Most towns have a website you can check, but if you're looking for that personal touch, the people at the local municipal offices can help. They know about all the services your town and county offer. Are you wondering about trash pickup? Town workers can tell you the schedule. And because the whole country is focusing more on **recycling**, towns are making it easy for **residents** by supplying special recycling containers. The Public Works Department is **responsible for** the care of all township property. Is there a **pothole** in your street? Call the department! Does your road flood in a **heavy rain**? Call the department! Do you need someone to take away all those piles of leaves you raked up? Call the department! Are you looking for parks and recreation? Call the department!

Oh, yeah, we all can use a little recreation. Take your pick! There are local **jogging trails** and **nature paths**. There are baseball fields and tennis courts. How about a **picnic** in the park while the **kiddies** are playing in the **tot lot**? Some parks even have a dog park. Yes, take your pooch along so he can play with his little doggie **pals**! Remember to take some **poop** bags. Owners need to clean up after their **mutts**.

Are you thinking about new activities with the neighbors? How about **yoga**? You can find boat safety classes and golf lessons. And most towns have special activities designed just for **seniors.** If someone you know is looking for **bus trips** and special **crafts** activities, just call your town office! You can even call the town for help with **stray** animals in the neighborhood or information about immunization shots for your cat. Count us out for that one—we're **dog people!** ☺

We're not kidding when we say your town and county offices can help you find anything at all you need. Even the police department offers great tips on how to keep your home safe. If you're going away (did somebody say *vacation*? Yay!), you can ask the police to drive by your street and **keep an eye on** things while you're gone. Local government offices also provide special programs and services for seniors and people with **disabilities**. And if you're wondering about how to **register** the kids for school, the town can direct you to the right school district. Back to school, kids! They're waiting for you!

## DIALOGUE 2: TRACK 37

**RECEPTIONIST:** Hi. Welcome to Slumberton Township. Can I help you?

**LIA:** Thanks, yeah. I think I've got a big problem. Now that the nice weather is here, I'm spending more time outside in the yard. The other day I noticed a cat with a **litter** of **kittens** in the corner of the yard under a tree.

**RECEPTIONIST:** I love kittens! They're so cute! Did you ask your neighbors if anyone is **missing** a cat?

**LIA:** Oh, I think kittens are cute, too. But I'm not crazy about them when they grow into cats. I'm a dog person. Anyway, I checked with the neighbors, but they don't own the cats. I don't know what to do about them. I don't really want a litter of kittens in my yard, but I don't know who can help me.

**RECEPTIONIST:** Come on in. Mr. Farkel is our **animal control officer**. His office is right down the hall, on the left. His department takes care of these things. I'm sure he can help.

**LIA:** That's a relief! I don't want them to **go hungry**, but I don't want the responsibility of taking care of them.

*** *a short time later* ***

**MR. FARKEL:** I understand that you have some **feral cats** in your yard. Be careful. These are wild cats, and they can be very **aggressive** around humans.

**LIA:** I don't want to hurt them. Is there some way to move them from my yard?

**MR. FARKEL:** Actually, we have a feral cat program. There are a few specially trained cat people in the neighborhood who can trap the cats **humanely**. Then they'll take them to a vet to be **neutered** or **spayed**. When the cats have **recovered**, they'll be **released** back into the woods.

**LIA:** Won't they be in danger in the woods?

**MR.FARKEL:** These cats can take care of themselves. They'll be fine.

**LIA:** Wow, thanks so much for the help. I didn't know there are so many ways the town can help residents!

---

**TIP 3**

One of the most important services offered in every city is education. Everyone who lives in the United States can have a *free* public school education. Kids start early, but the **cutoff** dates for birthdays **vary** from state to state:

- Pre-K is for children aged three and/or four. (The actual age depends on where you live. Pre-K is not **mandatory**.)
- Kindergarten is for five-year-olds.
- Elementary school starts at first grade.
- Middle school (sometimes called junior high) is usually for grades 6, 7, and 8.
- High school (also called secondary school) is for grades 9, 10, 11, and 12.

---

**TIP 4**

To register for school, people need to prove that they live in the town. These are the documents most schools districts require:

- Proof of the student's birth date
- A record of **immunizations**
- Proof that the student lives in the district
  - A copy of an apartment lease agreement
  - A copy of a utility bill (for example, water, telephone, or cable)
  - Parent's driver's license or another photo ID

# VOCABULARY

- **aggressive**: with a strong tendency to fight or hurt
- **animal control officer**: the person who makes sure owners register their pets; he or she also takes care of any animal issues in the town
- **bus trips**: activities that take groups of people to someplace special
- **confusing**: not clear
- **crafts**: things to make with simple materials
- **cutoff date**: the last day something will be allowed
- **disabilities**: needs that require special help (these can include problems walking, seeing, hearing, or learning)
- ⓘ **dog people/cat people**: people who prefer a certain pet
- **feral cats**: wild cats that live outdoors and have no human owners
- **go hungry**: be without food
- **heavy rain**: a lot of rain
- **humanely**: in a kind way that won't hurt
- **immunizations**: shots (injections) to prevent certain diseases
- **jogging trails**: paved paths for jogging (a form of running)
- ⓘ **keep an eye on**: watch in a protective way
- ⓘ **kiddies**: kids (Don't confuse this with *kitties*, which is another word for *kittens*, or baby cats.)
- **kittens**: baby cats (Baby dogs are called *puppies*.)
- **litter**: a group of cats or dogs born at the same time to the same mother
- **mandatory**: required
- **missing**: lost (Note this second meaning for *miss*; see the Dialogue 1 vocabulary list to refresh your memory about another meaning.)
- ⓘ **mutt**: a dog of mixed breeds
- **nature paths**: walkways through woods for exercise and enjoying nature
- **neutered** (for male animals): testicles removed in a painless medical procedure
- ⓘ **pal**: friend
- **picnic**: a special meal for eating in a park or other outside area
- ⓘ **poop**: Hmmm. How do we say this nicely? It's what comes out the tail end of your pooch. ICK!
- **pothole**: a hole in the middle of the street

- **recovered**: got better; get healthy again
- **recycling**: collecting bottles, cans, plastic, and paper to use again
- **register**: sign up; enroll
- **released**: set free
- **residents**: people who live in a place
- **responsible for**: have something be your job
- **seniors**: older people usually around 60 or more
- **services**: programs to make life easier or more comfortable
- **spayed** (for female animals): reproductive organs removed so they won't have more babies
- **stray**: an animal that is lost
- ⓘ **tons**: a lot
- ⓘ **tot lot**: children's playground in a park
- **vary**: be different
- **yoga**: a fitness program that stretches the body and calms the mind

## GRAMMAR REMINDER 3: More Present Continuous Tense

Hey, did you spot the present continuous tense again?
*I'm spending more time outside in the yard.*

Here it has a slightly different meaning. Rather than meaning "at this particular moment" (as in "I'm sending" in Dialogue 1), it means the *general* time frame around now. So Lia is not out in her yard right now (she is in the township office talking to Mr. Farkel!) but she is out in the yard more often, *in general*, around this time of year.

Remember those stative verbs (see unit 4)? Although she is talking about time *around* now, some verbs cannot be used in the continuous tense. Examples are the verbs *to know* and *to want*. They are stative verbs. Look at these examples from the dialogue.

| *Correct Examples:* | *Not:* |
| --- | --- |
| I don't know what to do about them. | I'm not knowing what to do about them. |
| I don't really want kittens in my yard. | I'm not really wanting kittens in my yard. |
| I don't know who can help me. | I'm not knowing who can help me. |

## MORE FUN WITH IDIOMATIC EXPRESSIONS:
## Take Your Pick

- **take your pick**: choose any one
  *She was first on line for the special sale, so she got to **take her pick** of the best dresses.*

- **pick up the check:** pay the bill for something
  *Sarah wanted to **pick up the check** when she took her dad to lunch.*

- **pick out**: choose; select
  *For his birthday, Tommy's mom let him **pick out** one special toy to buy.*

- **pick on**: tease; be mean to someone
  *The teacher stopped the little boy when he tried to **pick on** a smaller kid.*

- **pick and choose**: be selective; choose carefully
  *Antonio arrived at the flower shop when it opened, so he had plenty of time to **pick and choose** the perfect plant.*

- **pick up on**: understand, notice
  *It wasn't hard to **pick up on** the surprise; everyone was whispering when she walked in the door.*

### *Fun Fact!*
Okay, you know what's coming. What do we call that favorite vehicle with a large open space in back for carrying just about anything you need to move? Yes, it's a *pickup truck!*

# Culture Vulture

## What's Happening?

Home, sweet home. It's great to get mail and read all the news and gossip from home. As you're reading, are you listening to a favorite CD from the library? Are you thinking about how nice it would be to hear a concert in person? It's not hard to do. There are plenty of **opportunities** to hear **live music**, and many of them are right in the neighborhood. Are you interested in the arts? Pick up a copy of the local newspaper. The Arts and Entertainment section will have a full list of all the **cultural activities** going on in the area. There are activities to make every **culture vulture** happy. If you do some research, you can find out what days are "pay what you wish" at some famous museums. Instead of a **pricey** ticket, you can give what you feel you can **afford** that day. (Remember that museums are not open every day, and if you're hoping to see that **special exhibition** at the Museum of Modern Art, make sure it's open on the day you plan to go. And be sure to check the **hours**!)

In the newspaper, you'll be able to find theater **reviews**, **movie times**, and reviews of new **music releases**. Look for a section called Community Events. You'll find that most communities have **arts groups** that perform locally. There are plays, classical concerts, and popular music. Even the local high schools and colleges **put on** plays and concerts. Ticket prices for these local **performances** are usually very low, and the performers are often very talented, so you can bring the whole family. In fact, you can even **audition** to become part of an **orchestra**, **amateur theater group,** or **dance troupe.** Are you wondering what it would be like to be a star? Imagine having the **paparazzi** follow you all day! Wouldn't your neighbors love to see you performing onstage? We sure would!

If you live in the city or the suburbs, you're always pretty close to a live **professional** performance, too. Don't be **discouraged** if it seems that the tickets for these events are very expensive. Costs for professional orchestras and musicians are pretty high. But we have the **inside scoop** for you. You may not have to pay **full price** for those fancy tickets! Check to see if you can subscribe to a half-price ticket newsletter. This is a weekly listing of the plays, museums, and concerts that are offering **half-price** tickets. In our town, the list is delivered every week right to our e-mail box. You can get a great bargain without ever leaving your **couch**! But if you're **out and about** and visiting the city, places like New York City often have a special **kiosk** where you can buy these half-price tickets. Often, they're **good** only on the day of the performance, so get to the city early. Be sure to check for the hours of the ticket booths, too. And don't forget to check at the theater **box office** the day of the show. You can sometimes get a great deal there, too.

You've probably noticed that we use the word *theater* in a lot of different ways. For a special night out, someone may "go to the theater." This *always* means that they're going to see a **play**, and it *usually* means a Broadway show. This is not a TV show! A Broadway show is a play that is acted out by professional actors. It's professional theater. A Broadway show can also be a musical. That's a play that has lots of songs and many **dance numbers**. *Theater* also refers to the building. So *theater* can mean the show *and* the place where the show is performed!

But we're not finished yet! A theater can also refer to the place where you go to see a movie. So you go to your favorite movie theater to see a movie. **Film buffs** may say they're going to the **cinema**. They're talking about the movies in a fancy way. Film buffs often call movies *films*. You probably know that the **film industry** in the United States is mostly located in Hollywood, California. But did you know some people call Hollywood the "City of Broken Dreams"? Can you guess why? Imagine all the people who travel to Hollywood hoping to become rich movie stars. Only a very few ever become famous film stars. The rest live with their broken dreams . . .

## Fun Fact!

The Academy Award (the top prize in the United States for the film industry) is called the Oscar. It got its name from a librarian (yes!) who said that the award statue looked like her Uncle Oscar!

## DIALOGUE 1: TRACK 38

**ALAN:** Hi, Lia. What's happening?

**LIA:** Not much, Alan. But my cousin Bevin's coming to town this week, so I'm pretty excited.

**ALAN:** Cool. Are you planning to stay home and **catch up**, or are you going into the city? Is she staying for a while?

**LIA:** Well, she's not staying very long. But I really want to **show her around**, so I'm looking to see what's happening in the city this week. I know she'd like to see a show, so I'm hoping to get two-fers; you know . . . two tickets for the price of one . . . for a musical on Broadway. We're not worrying about which musical—any one will do!

**ALAN:** Are you thinking about eating in a restaurant, too? I think I have two-fers for a great Italian restaurant right near the theater district. I'm not going into the city for a while, so I'd be happy to give them to you.

**LIA:** Wow, that's pretty nice of you! I wanted to **treat** Bevin to a nice dinner, but I know those restaurants are pricey. But if we have a coupon to get two dinners for the price of one, I'm in! And I think I know the place you mean. I read a review of Luigi's Restaurant in Sunday's paper; the food critic said that it's excellent.

**ALAN:** Yeah, you'll have to make reservations before you go. Dinner and a show! Your cousin will have a great time.

**LIA:** I'll have a great time, too! I **can't wait!**

**TIP 1**

If you're a student, be sure to ask for the student price at cultural events. Most places offer a good discount for students. You may have to show your student ID. There are discounts for seniors too.

**TIP 2**

If your student days are over, you can still find a good deal at the local concert hall. Call to see if they have "Community Rush" tickets. This allows people to come to the box office on the day of the performance for cheap tickets. It's a good way to be sure everyone in the community can afford to see a good concert.

**TIP 3**

*Theater? Theatre?*
You'll see it spelled both ways. Take your pick!

## VOCABULARY

- **afford**: be able to pay for
- **amateur**: not for money
- **arts groups**: community groups of people with an interest in the arts
- **audition**: try out to become part of an event
- **box office**: the booth in the theater where you buy tickets
- ⓘ **can't wait**: be excited about something about to happen
- ⓘ **catch up**: learn all the news from someone
- **cinema**: another term for "movies"
- **couch**: sofa
- **cultural activities/the arts**: things to do with the arts, for example, music, dance, theater, and art
- ⓘ **culture vulture**: a person who is very interested in museums and the arts
- **dance numbers**: special routines in a show for dancers
- **dance troupe**: people putting on a dance performance
- **discouraged**: feeling bad
- ⓘ **film buff**: someone with a strong interest in everything about movies
- **film industry**: the business of making movies
- **full price**: paying the entire cost of each ticket
- **good**: valid, able to be used
- **half-price**: paying only half of the cost for each ticket
- **hours**: scheduled times something is open
- ⓘ **inside scoop**: the information only people who live there know
- **kiosk**: a small building where something is sold
- **live music**: music that you hear right there as they play it, not recorded

- **movie times**: times the movie will show at the theater
- **music releases**: days when new music goes on sale in stores
- **opportunities**: chances
- **orchestra**: a group of musicians playing many classical instruments
- ⓘ **out and about**: going to different places
- **paparazzi**: photographers who are always around looking for famous people
- **performances**: shows before an audience
- **play**: a drama intended for performance before an audience
- ⓘ **pricey**: expensive
- **professional**: an expert, someone who performs for pay
- ⓘ **put on**: perform before an audience
- **reviews**: an expert's report about something
- ⓘ **show someone around**: take a visitor to interesting places
- **special exhibition**: a special show that will be there for only a short time
- **theater group**: people putting on plays
- ⓘ **treat**: pay for, as a special event or reward

## GRAMMAR REMINDER 1: The Present Continuous Tense— Questions

To ask a question in the present continuous tense, remember to just switch the subject and present form of the verb *to be*: present form of **to be** → *subject* →-**ing** form of the main verb. (If needed, remember to put the question word at the beginning.) Look at the examples from the dialogue:

- **Are** *you* plann**ing** to stay home and catch up, or are you going into the city?
- **Are** *you* think**ing** about eating in a restaurant, too?
- **Is** *she* stay**ing** for a while?
- ***Where*** **is** *she* stay**ing?**

## *Fun Fact!*

Half-price tickets are often called *two-fers*. Can you guess why? They're priced so that you can buy two fer (for) the price of one!

## MORE FUN WITH IDIOMATIC EXPRESSIONS: Music

- **music to one's ears:** something great
  *She really missed her family a lot, so it was **music to her ears** when she heard her sister's voice.*

- **for a song**: for a very low price
  *The shop at the beach was closing for the winter, so she was able to buy a swimsuit **for a song**.*

- **face the music**: handle consequences of an action
  *She was unprepared for the meeting, so she had to **face the music** when her boss asked for a report.*

- **ring a bell**: sound familiar
  *He didn't recognize the professor's face, but her name **rang a bell**.*

- **sing someone's praises**: say very good things about someone
  *When he finally handed in an excellent report, the boss **sang his praises** to the whole department.*

# See the Capital . . . and the Capitol

Are you **dying to** see museums and historical monuments? If you have some time, head to Washington, D.C. A visit to our nation's **capital** is the culture bargain of a lifetime! The Smithsonian Institution is worth a trip from anywhere. Although even some Americans think that the Smithsonian is a single museum, in fact, it's a **complex** of 19 museums and 9 research centers. NINETEEN MUSEUMS! All of them right in the same area! And here's the best part: they're free! There is no admission fee to visit any of the Smithsonian museums. Yes, U.S. taxes pay for these museums, so you can enjoy seeing those taxes hard at work.

Do you like **bugs**? There's a museum for that. Thinking about flying to the moon? There's a museum for that. **Longing for** a look at **long-lost lizards**? There's a museum for that. The Smithsonian Institution has museums for just about anything you could possibly be interested in. Maybe you're just hoping for a stroll through beautiful gardens surrounded by **sculpture**. Yes, the Smithsonian has it all: **architecture** and art, gardens, space information, ethnic museums, collections of clothing, history . . . You name it, and it's there. And, of course, you can even buy a not-so-culturally-important T-shirt on the mall. In fact, when you need a rest from all that walking, the mall is a beautiful spot to relax. This is not a shopping mall; it's a long stretch of **lawn** and walkways, with benches and some food places. You can see the beautiful U.S. **Capitol** building with its white **dome** on one end, and the 555-**foot**-tall Washington Monument on the other end.

Because there's so much to do and see, it's a good idea to plan your cultural visit well in advance. If you're not planning to do a tour on foot, you can arrange for all kinds of different tours. These special tours will cost money. Of course, there are the typical bus tours. These will pick you up at many different locations and drive you through the entire area. Usually you can hop on and hop off. As the bus takes you to different spots, you can stop to visit the attraction for as long as you'd like, then get on a bus to the next stop when you're ready. Or you can take bicycle tours of the area. How about a **Segway** tour? Now, that is cool! There are tons of special tours you can book, according to your interests. Some of these are very popular, so you might want to buy your tickets in advance. You can do it online and avoid the wait at the tour office or ticket counter.

If you plan in advance, you can also **time your visit**. That way you can easily **fit in** all you want to see. Check online for museum **floor plans** and know what sections you plan to visit. (You can spend an entire day in some places and still not see everything!) See what other museums are nearby. Don't forget historical museums where you can learn all about the city, certain industries, and cultural and ethnic influences on the country.

And you will probably want to visit many of the beautiful **memorials** along the mall. There are several that honor past presidents, as well as many war memorials. These commemorate the sacrifices of people who served in the country's wars. Visiting these **monuments** and memorials is a nice way to think about all the wonderful things we have . . . and the people who made them possible.

Just make sure you leave plenty of time for **browsing** in the gift shops!

## DIALOGUE 2: TRACK 39

**LIA:** Hey, Alan, aren't you planning a trip to London this month?

**ALAN:** Well, that was the **original** plan. But now we're not planning to go to the UK at all. We've decided to save some money and just have a staycation this year.

**JAE:** Yeah. We're going to **Plan B**: just stay home and have a vacation doing things nearby. And with the money we save, we're planning to see three extra shows when we go to London next year! We're thinking about a drive to Washington, D.C., for a weekend. What do you think?

**LIA:** Wow, **road trip**! Count me in! The North Tower at the National Gallery has an **exhibit** of American art that I really want to see. And I'm **dying to** see the special Matisse paper cuttings exhibit. I checked the floor plan, and I see that they've moved it from the Tower to the **Concourse**. Every time I'm in the capital, I forget to plan around the exhibit's hours, and I miss it. Every time!

**ALAN:** Don't you check the museum's hours? Isn't it open all day?

**LIA:** Sure, I know the museum's hours. But the Matisse exhibit has its own hours, **separate from** the rest of the museum. Because the paper cuttings are **fragile**, they're only **on display** for certain times of the day. Too much light can damage them.

**JAE:** Well, we're not staying in D.C. very long, and we're planning to buy tickets for an **opera** performance at the Kennedy Center. I'm not sure we'll **get around to** going to the National Gallery of Art on this trip.

**LIA:** I know you culture vultures have your own plan. But we can save some big bucks if we **carpool** down. Then you can **do your own thing**, and I'll go see the Matisse exhibit. I'm not going home until I see that exhibit! We can **split the gas**, and we can **share the driving**. It'll be a great way to save money and have a great cultural weekend. And if you're lucky, maybe I'll sing on the way home!

**ALAN:** Aaghh! It sounds like a great idea, but we'll only do it if you promise *not* to sing!

**TIP 4**

Find out who the **congressional representative** is in your **voting district**. If you call that office a few weeks before you go, the representative can sometimes arrange a special tour of the White House for you! (Your friends will be very impressed.)

## VOCABULARY

- **architecture**: the art of designing buildings or other structures
- **browsing**: just looking around
- ⓘ **bugs**: insects
- **capital**: – spelled with an *a* – the city where the government is centered
- **capitol**: – spelled with an *o* – this is the office building where government business takes place
- **carpool**: join with other people for a drive
- **complex**: many things in one area
- **concourse**: the main area of a place, usually the first floor
- **congressional representative**: the person elected in a district to vote in Congress for laws that the people in the district want
- **dome**: a shape that looks like half a circle
- ⓘ **do your own thing**: separate so each person does what is interesting to him or her
- ⓘ **dying to**: want to do something very much
- **exhibit**: a special display in a museum or gallery
- ⓘ **fit in**: be able to see a lot of things
- **floor plan**: a map of where things are located in all areas of a place
- **foot**: a unit of measurement. Remember: we do not usually use the metric system in the United States.
- **fragile**: delicate and easily damaged
- ⓘ **get around to**: find time to do something

- **lawn**: a large grassy area
- **lizards**: reptiles of many sizes
- **longing for**: wanting very much
- ⓘ **long-lost**: something that hasn't been seen for a very long time
- **memorials, monuments**: buildings, gardens, or statues made to honor very important people or times in history
- **on display**: able to be seen
- **opera**: a musical play with all parts sung by professional classical singers
- **original**: first
- ⓘ **Plan B**: a second-choice plan
- ⓘ **road trip**: a fun trip taken in the car
- **sculpture**: art that is made by shaping or carving stone, clay, or some other material
- **Segway**: a cool two-wheeled scooterlike vehicle that is run by balancing; people stand on it (See the pronunciation note for another interesting /seg-way/.)
- **separate from**: different from
- ⓘ **share the driving**: take turns driving on a long trip
- ⓘ **split the gas**: share expenses of driving somewhere
- **time your visit**: plan your day so that you can see a lot of things
- **voting district**: the area that elects the person to act for the district in local, state and the national government; neighborhoods in towns may belong in different districts

## GRAMMAR REMINDER 2: The Present Continuous Tense—Negatives

To make a verb negative in the present continuous tense, just add *not*. Be sure to watch the word order! It goes like this: subject → present form of verb *to be* → *not* → *-ing* form of the main verb.

Can you find these examples from the dialogue?
- **We're not** plann**ing** to go to the UK. (We **aren't** planning to go to the UK.)
- **She's not** stay**ing** very long. (She **isn't** staying very long.)
- **I'm not** go**ing** home until I see that exhibit!

**Usage Reminder:** *What do you think* is an informal way of asking *What's your opinion?*

## PRONUNCIATION POINTER

You can impress your friends with a very fancy English word that means "to gently move from one topic to another." The word is **segue** and it is pronounced *seg-way*—just like the Segway that people can ride! (Maybe the inventor gave it this name because it moves people easily from one place to another?) Here's how **segue** can be used in a sentence: *They were talking about culture, but when the baseball player arrived, they* **segued** *[seg-wayed] into a discussion about sports.*

# Helping Out

## Helping Hands, Giving Back

Sometimes, the best way to make yourself at home in your new country is to **get involved** by **helping out** in the community. Actually, **volunteerism** is a very important value to Americans. We are aware that we have many advantages, and we value showing appreciation for this by sharing with others who may have less. **Giving back** doesn't only mean giving *things*.

It also means giving time, or sharing **talent**. The number of ways to help others is almost **limitless**. You might think, "I'm new here. What can I do?" Actually, newcomers have plenty to offer. In fact, the talents of people new to the United States have always been huge **assets** to the country. Your community needs you!

Where do you start? Well, what do you like to do? Do you sing in the shower? How about going to a **nursing home** and singing for the residents? They'll love it (well, we hope they'll love it), and if you sing in your native language, they may think you're a world famous **star**! Can you **knit**? Do you enjoy **carpentry**? Do you know a lot about plants and **landscaping**? Libraries and large stores are always looking for people to **demonstrate** special **skills** for small groups of people. This is a great way to practice your English! Do you have special job experience? Sometimes it's difficult to get the same kind of job in a new country that you had in your home country. A good way to **stay connected** is to volunteer in your **field**. Maybe you were in the health-care field. Hospitals and **care centers** would love to have you. Even if you just spend time talking to patients, you can **boost their morale**.

Don't forget that your language is a talent, too! Lots of times people come to a hospital or town office with no English language skills at all. Maybe you could volunteer to be a **go-between** and help them explain what they need. There are plenty of families that want their children to learn another language. If you offer to **tutor** a child, you may find that your English skills get better, too.

Do you know where everything is in your community? Can you find your way around? A great way to discover new places, roads, and neighborhoods is to volunteer to drive seniors or patients to appointments and treatment centers. **Homebound shut-ins** often need help with grocery shopping or meals. **Organizations** need people to help with **Meals-on-Wheels** and other food assistance programs.

You may have more talents than you realize!

## DIALOGUE 1: TRACK 40

**LIA:** Alan! Where are you **rushing off** to?

**ALAN:** Yikes! It's almost lunch time! I'm **running behind**!

**LIA:** Haha. You must really be hungry. I don't remember you ever **running around** like a crazy person just to go to lunch! Are you meeting some friends?

**ALAN:** Well, see, that's the thing. I'm not *eating* lunch. I'm *serving* lunch this afternoon.

**LIA:** Alan! I didn't know you got a job as a waiter! What restaurant are you working at? I'm going tonight, just to watch you **balancing trays**!

**ALAN:** No, no, no! I'm not working as a waiter, Lia. I'm serving lunch at the **soup kitchen** this afternoon, and later I'm working at the **food pantry**. I decided I wanted to do something to help people in the community, and a friend told me the Gilmore Street Food Pantry needed some help. I help out there **twice** a week.

**LIA:** Alan, what is the Gilmore Street Food Pantry?

**ALAN:** It's a great organization. They run a soup kitchen at the **homeless**

**shelter**, and twice a week the food pantry is open on Gilmore Street for families in need. I feel lucky that my family has enough food to eat, so it's an **honor** to help people who need some help while they're **getting back on their feet**. And talking to them helps me with my English. Maybe *they're* the ones who are doing the **good deed**.

If you're not an expert in something, but you'd still like to help, don't worry. Volunteer organizations will train you so you'll know exactly what to do.

Sometimes a volunteer job can lead to a real (paying!) job. Volunteering helps others, but organizations also need paid workers to help run everything. If you're really good at what you do, you may be offered a job in the organization.

## VOCABULARY

- **assets**: advantages
- **balancing**: holding something steady, so it won't fall
- **boost one's morale**: make someone feel better about things
- **care center**: a place where people's needs (usually health) are met
- **carpentry**: making beautiful things out of wood (or fixing them)
- **demonstrate**: show
- **field**: the industry or career you work in
- **food pantry**: a place that keeps food items on hand for families that need groceries but can't pay for them
- **get involved**: become a part of something
- ⓘ **getting back on one's feet**: trying to take care of one's own needs without help
- ⓘ **giving back**: helping someone else, because you're thankful for what you have
- ⓘ **go-between**: someone who works to help two groups understand each other and work together
- **good deed**: something kind that you do for someone
- ⓘ **helping out**: doing something to make things easier for someone
- **homebound shut-ins**: people who are sick and not able to leave their homes

- **homeless shelter**: a place where people with no homes can sleep
- **honor**: a privilege
- **knit**: make something by weaving yarn or thread (sweaters and scarves are knit)
- **landscaping**: arranging plants outside
- **limitless**: no end
- **Meals-on-Wheels**: a program that helps deliver food to people who need it
- **nursing home**: a place for older people who need extra care and help
- **organization**: a group that has a special purpose
- ⓘ **running around**: busy doing many things in a short time
- ⓘ **running behind**: late
- ⓘ **rushing off**: hurrying away
- **skill**: ability to do something well
- **soup kitchen**: a place that serves free meals to needy people
- **star**: a famous leader in an industry
- ⓘ **stay connected**: keep learning about your interest
- **talent**: a special ability
- **tray**: large flat board or plate for holding things (like plates and glasses in a restaurant)
- **tutor**: a special teacher for one person or a small group
- **twice**: two times
- **volunteerism**: the act of helping someone without expecting any pay or benefit

## *Fun Fact!*

We're not sure this is true, but some volunteers we've spoken to say they've lost ten pounds since starting their volunteer jobs. If that's true, sign us up!

## GRAMMAR REMINDER: Even More Present Continuous Tense

The present continuous tense (form of *to be* + *-ing* form of the verb) works very hard! Many people use the present continuous tense to talk about something that will happen in the near future.

Take a look at these examples from the dialogue (see if you can find any more).

**Are** you meet**ing** some friends?
I'**m not** eat**ing** lunch.
I'**m** serv**ing** lunch this afternoon.
I'**m** work**ing** at the food pantry.

## Good Citizen? Good Neighbor!

Helping out in the community is a great way to show respect for the people you live with, and volunteering is a wonderful way to be a good citizen. Of course, becoming an actual citizen of the country is a **legal process**. However, you don't have to be an actual citizen to be a good citizen. Being a good neighbor, friend, co-worker (you get the idea) is what U.S. citizenship is all about.

Perhaps the most **sacred document** to all U.S. citizens is the **U.S. Constitution**. This is the statement of all the rights and basic freedoms that every person is **entitled to**. It says, for example, that people have the right to **free speech.** But being a good American means using this right for good purposes and in the service of helping others. A good citizen will express his opinion on important issues, but he will also respect the opinions of others—even if those opinions are different from his. In fact, this may be the most important part of living in this country: using the rights and **privileges** that are ours as citizens to help all of the society we live in. Loving the country; respecting its laws; being part of the family, neighborhood, town—all of these show respect for the country that protects these rights for us.

Enjoying our rights as citizens is something that people should never **take for granted**. Because they were **hard-won**, and because there are so many who would be honored to have these rights, it's important that people **pay their dues**. Although *we* may be **firm** in what we believe, it's a citizen's duty to allow neighbors to keep their beliefs as well. Respecting people, respecting laws, and **acknowledging** responsibility and duty all **come with the territory**.

U.S. citizens should do all that their country asks of them. Becoming part of the process helps keep it strong. Citizens should vote, to express those opinions that they are free to have. We need to do our part to protect the environment. And while everyone likes to complain about them, paying taxes is what makes so many of our programs work. Even something as simple as **jury duty** is an important way to be a good member of the community. Rights and privileges are part of what makes this such a great country; people taking responsibility is what helps keep it strong.

## DIALOGUE 2: TRACK 41

**LIA:** Oh, no, I can't believe this. I just got a **notice** that I'm being called for jury duty.

**ALAN:** Wait a minute! Why "oh, no"? Don't you like the American jury system?

**LIA:** Oh, of course, I like the jury system. It's just such a **pain in the neck**. Now I have to take time off from work, I have to figure out how to get there, and I have to wait around until they call me in. Then if I **get picked** for a jury, who knows how long I'll have to spend in court? I don't have time for this! Why can't they just ask someone who has nothing better to do?

**ALAN:** Okay, it does take a commitment of time. But, Lia, what if someone you care about was **on trial**? Wouldn't you want them to have the best people possible **serving on the jury**?

**LIA:** I know, I know. You're right. I guess the best part about the court system is that someone can have her case heard by a jury of her **peers**. It just seems like there's never enough time to do everything.

**ALAN:** I know. Everyone wants to have the privileges and advantages of something, as long as he doesn't have to make any effort. If everyone **stepped up to the plate** and did his part, it would be a much fairer system for everyone. Even the people with "important" jobs need to make a **contribution** to society and be good citizens.

**LIA:** You're right. If I want to **take advantage of** all the good things that I have in this country, I should at least take my turn at sharing some of the responsibility. That's it. I'm calling them this afternoon and I'm telling them I'll be happy to do my jury duty.

**ALAN:** Great! Now let's go get lunch.

**TIP 3**

One very important right enjoyed by a citizen in our democracy is the right to have a jury decide his guilt or innocence. Sometimes a person may ask to have the judge make the final decision instead; then there will be no jury at the **trial**.

# VOCABULARY

- **acknowledging**: recognizing
- **burst**: pop, break
- ⓘ **comes with the territory**: is expected
- **contribution**: do something helpful to make a difference
- **document**: an official paper
- **entitled to**: have the right to something
- **firm**: strong
- **free speech**: the right of people to say whatever they want
- ⓘ **get picked**: be selected for something
- ⓘ **get the hang of**: be able to do something easily; understand something
- **hard-won**: achieved after much sacrifice by oneself or others
- **jury**: the group of people who hear all the arguments in a court case; they make the decision about who is right and wrong
- **jury duty**: serving in the court system as a member of the jury
- **legal process**: steps to make something happen as required by law
- **notice**: an official letter informing you of something
- **on trial**: in court to decide whether something is right or wrong
- ⓘ **pain in the neck**: an annoyance; an inconvenience
- ⓘ **pay one's dues**: work hard to deserve something
- **peers**: people just like you
- **privileges**: a special benefit
- **sacred**: very important and deserving respect
- **serving on a jury**: being part of the court system as a jury member
- ⓘ **stepped up to the plate**: accepted responsibility for something and act
- **take advantage of**: use and enjoy
- **take for granted**: accept something as what you deserve without valuing it
- **trial**: a court proceeding to decide if someone is guilty or innocent of a crime
- **U.S. Constitution**: the highest law of the United States and the basis of the entire government

## PRONUNCIATION POINTER

For speakers of some languages, the letters *B* and *V* can be very difficult to **get the hang of**. The letter *B* requires that the lips touch. For the letter *V*, the top front teeth should touch the bottom lip. Try these tongue twisters for practice. Good luck!

**V and B Tongue Twisters**
Betty bought a biscuit, but the baby bit it.
On her vacation, Vera drove a van to visit Uncle Vanya in his village.
Bobby bought a big balloon in Baltimore, but it **burst**.
Vinny volunteered to vacuum for Violet while she voted.

## MORE FUN WITH IDIOMATIC EXPRESSIONS: Run/Running

* **running behind**: late
  *Her alarm clock didn't wake her on time, so she was **running behind**.*

* **running the show**: being in charge
  *He spent so much time working at the food pantry that he was soon **running the show** when the leader became sick.*

* **running scared**: being worried that you'll lose at something
  *After they lost two games to the Colorado Rockies, the Philadelphia Phillies were **running scared** in the baseball series.*

* **run it by me again**: repeat something
  *I didn't hear what the speaker said about my car. Can you **run it by me again**?*

* **running around in circles**: seeming to be doing a lot of activity, but not getting anything accomplished
  *Instead of concentrating on one job at a time, she tried to do everything at once and was just **running around in circles**.*

# Review: Units 13–15

## VOCABULARY

*Fill in the missing letters to make the words needed in the sentences below.*

1. I don't need a new car. My old one is very r_ l_ _ _ _ _ and never breaks down.

2. Hey, Toby, I've got some GREAT _ _ss_ _ for you. Julie in the office is getting married to Bob!
   NO! I thought she hated him!

3. Hey, Chris, I'm spending a lot of time on my new _ _ bb_.
   Bungee jumping?
   No! Stamp collecting. It's really relaxing.

4. Aaack! I drove too fast over a p_ t _ _ _ _ in the road, and now I've got a flat tire.

5. My dog just had a _ _ tt _ _ of eight puppies!

6. My husband is a really good golfer.
   Is he a professional?
   No, he's just an a _ _ t _ u _. But he's almost as good as a professional.

7. The worst thing about being famous is being followed everywhere by p _ _ _ _ _ zz_ trying to get photos of you on a bad hair day.

8. I hate to be outside in the summer time. I get eaten alive by the _ u _ s.

9. Be careful with that glass vase. It's very old and f_ _ g _ _ _.

10. Do you like my sweater? I've been learning to k _ _ _ , and I made it myself.

## INFORMAL LANGUAGE

*Can you explain these expressions? Try using them in a sentence.*

11. scope out
12. give someone a hand
13. grab a quick bite
14. keep an eye on
15. pricey

16. catch up
17. treat to
18. dying to
19. Plan B
20. running behind

## GRAMMAR

*Choose the correct preposition of place from above the map to complete the sentences below.*

near        between        on        in        in

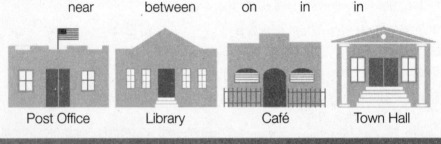

Post Office     Library         Café          Town Hall

Holly Street

Movie Theater   Mexican Restaurant   Chinese Restaurant   Italian Restaurant

22. There are a lot of restaurants _____ this neighborhood.

23. The town hall is _____ this block.

24. The Mexican restaurant is _____ the middle of the block.

25. The Chinese restaurant is _____ the movie theater.

*Look at the following sentences.*

✓ Put a check next to the sentences that are correct.

✗ Put an X next to the sentences that are incorrect. Can you underline the error and explain why it's wrong?

26. I'm not wanting fries with my burger. Could I have a side salad instead, please?

27. I meet some friends this afternoon.

28. We read a really good book at our book club this month.

29. You are meeting your friends this afternoon?

30. I'm not going shopping tonight; I'm too tired.

## The Dating Game

So you're in a **bar** and someone **catches your eye**. Wow, she's the girl of your dreams! You begin **chatting her up**, and soon you realize you're crazy about her. You want to **get together** the next evening and **go out** on a **date**. No, no, no! We're not talking about the fruit kind of date, or the what-day-is-it kind of date. We're talking about the **romantic** kind of date. How do you ask her? Where do you go? Well, don't ask us. It seems like hundreds of years since we've been on a date, and we've completely forgotten what to do. A date for us is a trip to the local supermarket. But our **sources** tell us there are many options to suit any pocketbook. How about **cocktails** at the local bar? Make sure you both have ID; you will probably be **carded.** How about a romantic **stroll** in the park? And, **just to be on the safe side**, make sure you know whom you are going with.

What if you never seem to meet anyone? These days, many people try **dating services** on the Internet to find **Mr. or Ms. Right**. Watch out for those **blind dates**, though. That 20-year-old **stunner** whose picture you saw may turn out to look more like your great-grandmother . . . or worse! Some people prefer to go on a **double date** at first until they feel more comfortable. Watch out at night; **cougars** could be **prowling** the streets! No, we're not talking about a big cat that has escaped from the zoo. Cougars are older women looking for younger men to date. (We think men must have come up with that comparison, haha.) And for you ladies, **sugar daddies** are not giant candy bars. These are older men looking for younger women to date. Be careful that you don't turn out to be some guy's **trophy wife**. Some rich old men just like the idea of going to events and parties with **arm candy.**

For kids in high school, one of the most important and exciting dates is **prom night.** This is a special evening with a very fancy dance that has music and food. If you're a parent, you'd better start saving. This can be an expensive time, with kids **going all out** to make it a perfect night. Girls spend lots of money on a special dress, a fancy hairstyle, and lots of makeup, and yes, some parents even rent a **limo** for the night. Here's the funny thing about prom night: however carefully you choose a dress and do your hair, you can be sure that in 30 years you'll **cringe** when you look at the pictures of yourself—and probably your date, too!

## DIALOGUE 1: TRACK 42

**ALAN:** Hi, Lia. What's up?

**LIA:** Oh, nothing much. Just trying to get ready for midterm exams.

**ALAN:** Mmm. Me, too. I'm feeling a little stressed.

**LIA:** Yes! I can't wait 'til they're over; then I can **let my hair down** a bit.

**ALAN:** Well, I could really use a **break** right now. Do you feel like **catching a movie** tonight? *Crazy Weekend with the Zombies* is playing at the **multiplex**.

**LIA:** Hey, that's a great idea! I'm dying to see that. I hear it's **hilarious**. Why don't we grab something to eat beforehand? I'm **sick of dorm food**.

**ALAN:** Sure. How about if I pick you up at about 7? The movie starts at 8:30, and we can grab a quick bite before we go.

**LIA:** Sounds great! See you at 7.

**TIP 1** Don't forget: you must be 21 to buy alcohol in the United States. Most places will card you. In some states, you can buy alcohol only in a liquor store. In others, you can buy beer and wine in a supermarket.

**TIP 2** Smoking is not allowed in most public places. Most smokers can be seen roasting in the summer and freezing in the winter as they stand outside a building for their smoke. Take our advice: it's much easier (and healthier) to quit (or never take it up in the first place)!

## VOCABULARY

- ⓘ **arm candy**: someone very attractive that you bring on a date to get attention
- • **bar**: a place for socializing that serves alcoholic beverages
- ⓘ **better half**: a fun term that refers to your partner in a serious relationship, or your spouse
- • **blind dates**: when you go out with someone before you've met him or her
- ⓘ **break**: a short time away from some stressful work
- ⓘ **carded**: asked to show identification that proves you are old enough to order alcohol
- ⓘ **catching a movie**: going to a movie (can also be used in other contexts, such as, *catching a baseball game, catching a show*)
- ⓘ **catches your eye**: is attractive to you; gets your attention
- ⓘ **chatting someone up**: having a casual conversation
- • **cocktails**: special alcoholic drinks with several ingredients
- ⓘ **cougars**: older women looking for young men to date
- • **cougars** (also called **mountain lions** or **pumas**): large wild cats, formerly found in many places in the United States but now rarely seen
- • **cringe**: be shocked or embarrassed at something
- • **date**: Four meanings here! (1) a fruit from the date palm tree; (2) a day on the calendar, like Monday, August 6; (3) a romantic event, time spent with someone special; (4) the person you go on a date with (So *date* can be the event and the person! Confused? That's English for you!)
- • **dating services**: groups (usually online) where you can sign up and look for people with similar interests

- ⓘ **dorm**: short for *dormitory*; the place where students live at a school or college
- **dorm food**: the kind of food served in schools
- **double date**: four people (two couples) going to the same place together
- ⓘ **get together**: meet with someone
- ⓘ **going all out**: spending lots of time and energy to make something perfect
- ⓘ **go out**: meet and spend time with someone
- **hilarious**: very funny
- ⓘ **just to be on the safe side**: being cautious with someone or something new
- ⓘ **let one's hair down**: relax
- **limo**: a very large, very fancy car that holds many people (or one rich movie star!)
- ⓘ **Mr. or Ms. Right**: the perfect person for you!
- **multiplex**: a movie theater that shows many different movies
- **prom night**: the most exciting social event for kids in high school
- **prowling**: searching for something; moving quietly like a cat
- **romantic**: about love
- ⓘ **sick of**: tired of
- **sources**: people who give you information
- **stroll**: a slow, enjoyable walk
- ⓘ **stunner**: someone who is very beautiful
- ⓘ **sugar daddy**: an older man who buys lots of presents for a younger woman he wants to date
- ⓘ **trophy wife**: a young beautiful woman who marries a much older, very successful (usually rich!) man

## PRONUNCIATION POINTER

Adding an *e* to the end of a word makes the *a* vowel sound long:
date = ***dayt***.

Say these pairs of words and notice how the *e* at the end makes the *a* sound longer:

| | | |
|---|---|---|
| Hat–hate: | *hat* | ***hayt*** |
| Rat–rate: | *rat* | ***rayt*** |
| Mat–mate: | *mat* | ***mayt*** |

## Will You Marry Me?

After you've been going out for a while, you may realize you **only have eyes for** that special person. Yes, you have **fallen for** her **big time** and decide that you want to to **get hitched.** First of all, you need to **pop the question.** Some people think it seems **old-fashioned** now, but it's still usually the custom for the man to **propose** to the woman. And what is the question? It's always, "Will you marry me?" Some guys get very creative and post the question on highway **billboards.** Some plan to do it at a sports event. But the really traditional marriage proposal is done on **bended knee,** after asking the woman's father for permission. If the woman says, "Yes, I will marry you!" you're **engaged!** She is your **fiancée,** and you are the **fiancé.** (We've taken these words from French. Don't ask us why, but it does sound romantic.)

Now you get to prepare for **the big day** when you will finally **tie the knot** and say, **"I do."** It's just about the best time of your life—and also the most stressful! Trying to have your dream wedding, keep all the **in-laws** happy, and stay within a **budget** can be a real chore. Things become even more interesting if you come from a family where parents have remarried. Now there are **stepparents** as well. Some people have a **wedding planner** to help them with the details. The great part about that is that the wedding planner gets to have the headaches! The planner does the **grunt work**, while the happy couple enjoys thinking about

**exchanging vows**. Well, they think about the vows . . . and about how they're going to pay the wedding planner!

A very popular custom with couples today is to set up a **bridal registry.** The bride-to-be registers with a store, and the couple decides what things they'd like in their new home. The best part? The bride and groom pick out all the cool stuff, but they don't have to spend a penny! They make a list of things they'd really like to have; friends and family check the list and decide what they'd like to buy as a gift. It sure **beats running the risk** of getting four toasters! Remember to include items in a **range** of prices. Some people may like to **chip in together** and get a more expensive gift. Other people may want to **go solo** and get something smaller.

Friends of the **bride** and **groom** often have **bachelor** or **bachelorette** parties to celebrate. This is the last chance to party with your friends as a single person. Don't **overdo** it and feel sick on your wedding day. Or worse: don't run off and **elope** with someone else!

Finally, the big day arrives, and it's all you ever dreamed it would be. The bride looks beautiful, the groom is handsome, and the guests are all well behaved. A success! Now, it's off to the **honeymoon** to **de-stress** from it all. Whew, what a **whirlwind**! Now all you have to do is *remember* the **anniversary,** or you'll be in big trouble!

## *Fun Fact!*

A bachelor party is called a **stag** party. We don't care what they're called: they're the parties when you kiss your single days good-bye!

### DIALOGUE 2: TRACK 43

**LIA:** It's my wedding anniversary tonight.

**JAE:** Oh, congratulations!

**LIA:** Yeah, gosh, it **takes me back** to when Tony first asked me to marry him. He had it all planned out so carefully.

**JAE:** Uh-oh. Sounds like there is a romantic story here.

**LIA:** It's quite a story, all right. He was working in New York, and I was still living in England, so I flew to New York City to spend a long weekend with him. We went to the top of the Empire State Building . . .

**JAE:** . . . and he asked you to marry him? With the stars **twinkling** in the night sky? There, at the top of the building, with the beautiful **skyline** of New York City right below you?! How romantic!

**LIA:** Um, well, uh, not quite. Yes, in his **original plan** he was going to ask me there. But . . . .

**JAE:** But . . . ?

**LIA:** Well, we had some friends with us, and Tony told his **bff** about the romantic Empire State Building proposal plan. His friend **begged** him not to propose to me there!

**JAE:** Are you kidding? Why not?

**LIA:** Tony's friend was with *his* girlfriend, too. He was worried that if Tony asked me to marry him, then his girlfriend would expect a proposal, too!

**JAE:** HAhahahaha! So then what happened?

**LIA:** Well, then Tony went to Plan B. He was going to take me out for a romantic meal at one of those Japanese restaurants where they prepare the food at the table. He was going to ask the guy to put my ring in the food.

**JAE:** Hahaha! This is too funny! Okay, so why didn't that happen?

**LIA:** I was so **jet-lagged** I didn't want to go out for dinner.

**JAE:** Just as well. You'd probably have eaten the ring. I can see you **choking** on your **engagement ring**. Help! Call 911! I've eaten an engagement ring!

**LIA:** Oh, very funny. Anyway, we ended up going out to a **bagel** place.

**JAE:** OH NO! Don't tell me he stuck the ring in the cream cheese, and then you couldn't find it!

**LIA:** Oh, just stop it. It may have been a little bagel place, but it could have been the fanciest, most elegant candlelit restaurant. He offered me the most beautiful ring and asked, "Will you be my wife?"

**JAE:** Did he get down on one knee? I hope he didn't **slip** on the cream cheese.

**LIA:** STOP IT! No, it wasn't on bended knee, but it was very romantic anyway. I'll never forget it. Okay, so how about you? What's your romantic proposal story?

**JAE:** You want a romantic story? Oh, I have a perfect romantic story.

**LIA:** Okay, I'm **all ears.**

**JAE:** Well, we were sitting next to a peaceful lake at sunset on a perfect summer day. The sky was **ablaze** with beautiful reds and orange, and some ducks went swimming by. Suddenly, on the dock below, a group of violins began to play. Jim got down on one knee and said, "You are the most wonderful thing in my life. Will you marry me and be my princess?"

**LIA:** That is so perfect! It's almost like a **fairy tale**!

**JAE:** Ha, ha. I know.   It *is* like a fairy tale! And, as you know, fairy tales are **make-believe**. You wanted a romantic story, that's what you got—a story! Okay, so it's *not* true, but the *real* story is pretty funny.  I'll save it for when we have a lot more time.

Don't forget to **RSVP** to an invitation! The bride needs to know exactly how many people to plan for at the **reception**, so it's important to **reply** and let her know if you'll be coming.

The invitation will usually say exactly who is invited. If the bride would like you to bring your boyfriend, the invitation will say "Miss Smith *and guest*."

## VOCABULARY

- **ablaze**: on fire, or seeming so
- ⓘ **all ears**: be listening very carefully
- **anniversary**: the date each year marking the wedding date (Your wife wants flowers!)
- **bachelor**: an unmarried man
- **bachelorette**: an unmarried woman
- **bagel**: a small, firm, circular bread (especially popular for breakfast in New York City)
- ⓘ **beats**: is better than
- **begged**: asked in a very strong way
- **bended knee**: getting down on one knee; usually this means the person is asking for something
- ⓘ **bff**: <u>b</u>est <u>f</u>riend <u>f</u>orever (Find this and other fun text shortcuts in Unit 19.)
- ⓘ **the big day**: a well-planned, exciting day
- ⓘ **big time**: enthusiastically
- **billboard**: large advertisement signs near a highway
- **bridal registry**: a list of items the couple needs to start a home
- **bride**: the woman on her wedding day

- **budget**: a money plan
- ⓘ **chip in together**: put money together to get a nice gift
- **choking**: getting something caught in your throat so that you're unable to breathe
- ⓘ **de-stress**: relax
- **elope**: get married in secret
- **engaged**: promised to marry
- **engagement ring**: a traditional gift from a man to a woman when he asks to marry her (In the United States, this is often a diamond ring.)
- **exchanging vows**: making promises to each other at the wedding
- **fairy tale**: a children's story about beautiful people and happy endings
- ⓘ **fallen for**: be in love with someone you've met
- **fiancé**: the man who will be married
- **fiancée**: the woman who will be married
- ⓘ **get hitched**: get married
- ⓘ **go solo**: do something alone
- **groom**: the man on his wedding day
- ⓘ **grunt work**: the hard work that no one wants to do
- **hen:** a female chicken
- **honeymoon**: a special vacation right after the wedding ceremony
- **"I do"**: the promise husbands and wives make to be faithful and good spouses
- **in-laws**: your spouse's family
- **jet-lagged**: the feeling of being tired after a long flight from another time zone
- ⓘ **make-believe**: pretend; not real
- **old-fashioned**: traditional; not modern
- ⓘ **only have eyes for someone**: be so in love that you can't think about anyone else
- ⓘ **original plan**: what you decide to do in the beginning (before going to Plan B!)
- **overdo**: do something too much
- ⓘ **pop the question**: ask someone to marry you
- **propose**: ask someone to marry you
- **range**: from one spot on a list to the opposite

- **reception**: a special party held after a wedding ceremony; also a party for other important events
- **reply**: respond; answer
- **RSVP**: thanks once again to the French!  This means: _Répondez, S'il Vous Plâit_  (please reply)
- **running the risk**: making a bad result possible
- **skyline**: the view of a city's buildings from a distance
- **slip**: fall on something wet or oily
- ⓘ **stag**: an animal with large antlers; a social gathering for men only
- **stepparents**: people who have married your biological parent
- ⓘ **takes me back**: reminds me of the past
- ⓘ **tie the knot**: get married
- **twinkling**: sparkling; lights blinking on and off
- **wedding planner**: someone whose job is to figure out all the details of the wedding
- **whirlwind**: a very fast, exciting time

### Fun Fact!

Traditionally, an American bride wears "something old, something new, something borrowed, something blue." Another tradition: a penny in the bride's shoe means good luck!

## MORE FUN WITH IDIOMATIC EXPRESSIONS: Love

- **a match made in heaven**: a perfect relationship
  _Tony and Jane's marriage was **a match made in heaven**. They were perfect for each other._

- **the love of one's life**: the one person you'll love forever
  _Peggy and Russ celebrated their 60th wedding anniversary; they both said, "You're still **the love of my life**!"_

- **head over heels**: absolutely and completely in love
  _Tina is **head over heels in love** with Jorge; she can't stop talking about him._

- **love at first sight**: falling in love with someone the very first time you see them
  _I knew Tom was the man I'd marry. It was **love at first sight** when we met in college._

- **on the rocks**: when a relationship starts to have problems
  *I think our neighbors' marriage is **on the rocks**. All I do is hear them fighting.*

- **kiss something good-bye**: have no chance of getting or doing something; to know that something is over or gone forever
  *Russ was ready to **kiss his bachelor days good-bye** when he popped the question to Peggy.*

## It's Over!

Ah, it was a beautiful relationship while it lasted. But not every couple is lucky enough to enjoy **wedded bliss** forever. Sometimes the problems that come up are too difficult to solve, and divorce seems like the only answer. So, after trying to **work things out** with your **spouse**, you've decided that you're at the **end of your rope**. It's not only that the two of you have **grown apart**, it's that you just can't **put up with** those smelly feet any longer! You've **given it your best shot**, but you **can't stand the sight** of those dirty socks all over the bedroom floor any longer. Or maybe it's something more serious. Maybe you've learned that your partner has been **cheating on** you and **having an affair**. After talking through all your options, you decide that the only solution is to **split up**. This is usually a sad decision, and many times couples will decide to give it a **second chance** and **get back together**. If the problems remain, and the couple just can't work things out, it may be the **end of the road** and, sadly (or happily?), time to say good-bye and get a **divorce**.

## DIALOGUE 3: TRACK 44

**LIA:** Hey, what's the matter? You **look down**.

**JAE:** Yeah, I guess I am. I just **broke up** with Josep.

**LIA:** You and Josep have broken up? Oh, no! What happened? I thought things were going really well.

**JAE:** Yes and no. He is such a nice guy in a lot of ways, but things just started getting really boring, you know. He stopped doing all the nice stuff like buying me flowers and saying nice things. He only wants to sit on the couch and watch TV, and I want to do fun things with friends.

**LIA:** I know what you mean; Tony is the same. I'd just like him to be a little more . . . well, romantic or something.

**JAE:** Yeah, but it's not only that. We've just **gone in different directions**. He isn't interested at all in any of the things I like to do. I just feel he has really **let me down.** I just can't **count on** him anymore.

**LIA:** Wow, I'm so sorry to hear that. I hope you **get over** the **breakup** soon. But after all, maybe there's still a chance that you two can work things out and **make up.** Maybe you should **put off** the **separation.**

**JAE:** Well, we've been trying for a long time, so I think this is the **end of the road** for us. But thanks anyway.

**TIP 5**

Before a couple decides to separate or divorce, they will often try **counseling.** A professional counselor who helps couples resolve their differences is called a marriage **therapist** or family therapist.

## VOCABULARY

- ⓘ **break up** (verb): end a relationship
- • **breakup** (noun): the situation when two people end a relationship
- ⓘ **can't stand the sight of**: hate something
- ⓘ **cheating on**: being unfaithful to a husband or wife
- • **counseling**: talking with a professional about how to solve problems
- ⓘ **count on**: depend on; rely on
- • **divorce**: a legal ruling that a marriage is officially over
- ⓘ **end of the road**: the last part of an experience
- ⓘ **end of your rope**: not having any more patience in a bad situation
- ⓘ **get back together**: reunite after a separation
- ⓘ **get over**: no longer be upset by a bad situation
- ⓘ **give it your best shot**: try your hardest at something
- ⓘ **go in different directions**: follow different interests; grow apart
- ⓘ **grow apart**: no longer like the same things
- • **having an affair**: cheating on a husband or wife, usually with the same person and for a long time
- ⓘ **let someone down**: disappoint someone

ⓘ **look down**: seem sad or unhappy

ⓘ **make up**: forgive and be friends again

ⓘ **put off**: postpone

ⓘ **put up with**: have patience; ignore something annoying

• **second chance**: another try to make things work

• **separation**: a time before a divorce when a couple isn't living together

ⓘ **split up**: separate; no longer be together

• **spouse**: the person someone is married to

• **therapist:** a professional who helps with problems

ⓘ **wedded bliss**: a fun way to talk about marriage as perfect happiness

ⓘ **work things out**: try to solve problems

## GRAMMAR REMINDER 1: Phrasal Verbs

Phrasal verbs are really common in informal English. They are verbs and particles (could be a preposition or adverb) that work together to change the meaning of the verb. It sounds more complicated than it is, and there aren't many English speakers who can tell you what a particle is anyway! Just know that they're **words that work together to make one meaning**.

• Some phrasal verbs are pretty easy to understand because they mean exactly what they say (literal):
> **go out** (which is, of course, going out of the house somewhere)
> *We **go out** to the movies every Friday night.*

• Others are trickier because there is no way you can figure out what they mean just by knowing all the words:
> **make up**
> *In a good relationship, it's important to **make up** after a disagreement.*

This is not to be confused with the noun *makeup* (one word), which means cosmetics. Isn't English *fun*?!

• Some phrasal verbs are separable, which means you can separate the verb from the particle:
> **let down**
> *Tom is never around to help when I need him.*
> *He **lets** me **down** all the time.*

- Some phrasal verbs are inseparable, which means you can't separate the verb and particle.

    **go out**
    *We **go out** together every weekend.*
    Never *say, We **go** together **out**.*

- Some phrasal verbs are transitive, which means they need a direct object.

    **put off**
    *You should **put off** the separation.*
    Never say, *You should **put off**. You must put off something*!

- Some phrasal verbs are intransitive, which means no direct object is necessary.

    **make up**
    *Maybe you two will **make up**.*
    Nothing else is needed.

Okay, so how do you **figure** all this **out**? (*Figure out* is another phrasal verb!) Okay, we admit it's tricky.

- Try to learn phrasal verbs in context as you hear them.
  The more you practice, the easier they become. We promise!
  If all else fails, **look** them **up** in a dictionary.

Ha! Did you spot it? **Look up,** used in this way, is a nonliteral, separable, transitive phrasal verb! We bet you already knew that . . .

## GRAMMAR REMINDER 2: Suggestions and Proposals

There are lots of ways to make suggestions and proposals. Watch the verb form that you need to use with each one.

**Informal**
- Verb + -*ing*:
  Do you feel like go**ing** out?
  How about go**ing** out?

- Base form of the verb:
  Let's **go** out.
  Why don't we **go** out?

**More formal**
**Will you** marry me?
**Would you** be my wife?
**Will you** be my princess? (Ha, ha. Good luck with that one.)

## PRONUNCIATION POINTER

The letter *o* can have different sounds. It all depends on what other letters come before and after it.

- *oh*, as in the word *toe*
- *oo*, as in the word *two*
- *ow*, as in the word *now*
- *uh*, as in the word *love*

Don't you love a vowel that can do all that?!

# That's Life!

New Life

## And Baby Makes Three

Yes, if you're doing the math, it very often **turns out** that, in relationships, one plus one equals three. What could be better: a new country, a new relationship, a new job, a new home, and now a new baby! **Starting a family** can be an exciting (and **nerve-racking**!) experience. It's also lots of fun. Okay, maybe the **mom-to-be** isn't having so much fun when she has **morning sickness** each day.

For many women, one of the most exciting times in life is when they learn that they are **pregnant**. Suddenly, there are plenty of things to think about. **Prenatal** care is really important. In the first place, a doctor will **calculate** the baby's **due date** pretty **accurately**. It's fun to wonder if the **new arrival** will come on Halloween or Christmas Day. Mom must be sure she stays healthy and makes healthy choices. After all, now she's **eating for two**. **Expectant mothers** have tons of questions, and the best person to give the answers is her **OB/GYN**. This doctor is usually just called an *OB* or *obstetrician*. The obstetrician will recommend **avoiding** all alcohol. If the mom-to-be is a smoker, the doctor will **definitely recommend** quitting. The doctor can also answer questions about what foods are best to eat, what medicines are safe to take, what vitamins are good to take, and how much exercise is okay. Some moms even have questions about how safe it is to be around the family pet! Good prenatal care makes sure that the baby will have the best, healthiest start to life.

Women in the United States have many choices about the type of childbirth they want. Although in the past women **relied on** doctors (usually men!) to make all the decisions about their childbirth, women today are far more **vocal** about how they want their baby to be born. And doctors (often women!) are happy to support a woman's choice. There are **deliveries** that involve medical procedures performed by a doctor and drugs to ease the process, and others that are called *natural* deliveries because they have less involvement of a doctor and fewer drugs.

Sometimes, in a **vaginal birth**, the mother may choose certain drugs to ease the pain. Not all women wish to have these drugs, however. Some choose vaginal delivery with no drugs at all. (Of course, they may change their minds once the **labor** pains start!) A popular approach to childbirth is the **Lamaze method**, which emphasizes special ways of breathing and ways to focus on special thoughts in order to manage the pain.

Some women don't like the idea of a medical delivery at all. They may choose to have the baby at home or in a special **birthing center** that is made to look like a comfortable home rather than a medical center. In these cases, the birth is often managed by a **midwife**. A midwife is not a doctor but a licensed caregiver who has had training in the birth process. A midwife can guide a normal delivery, but some state laws may require her to be in a hospital or special birthing center. If there is an emergency, everyone wants mom and baby to have immediate medical care from a doctor.

Everyone hopes a delivery will **go smoothly**. But sometimes emergencies happen, and a doctor may have to help in the process. Sometimes a **forceps** delivery may be necessary for a difficult birth. And in a real emergency, a doctor may have to perform a **Caesarean section**. This is a surgical procedure, commonly called a C-section, in which the baby is delivered through an **incision** in the mother's abdomen. Because it's **surgery**, the new mother must **recover** in the hospital for a few days.

Are you wondering where Dad is in all this? In **the old days**, Dad would be out in a waiting area, nervously **pacing back and forth**, just waiting to hear if his baby has been born. Not anymore! **Nowadays**, Dad is a very **hands-on** assistant in the whole process. Of course, Mom has the real job, but Dad will help out by trying to keep her comfortable through all the **stages of labor**. Most of the time, Dad will be in the **delivery room**, and he'll hold his new baby as soon as it's born.

Sure. Mom does all the work, and Dad has all the fun.

**JAE:** Lia, I'm so excited about your happy news! When are you due?

**LIA:** I know, I know! Can you believe it? I'm going to be a mom again! The OB says our little darling should arrive on December 8. And she says it could be **twins**!

**JAE:** What!? Twins? Do twins **run in the family**?

**LIA:** Yes, my husband is a twin and so is his mother!

**JAE:** Wow, when will you know for sure?

**LIA:** Well, the doctor's going to do an **ultrasound** at my next **visit**. We'll know for sure then. We'll also know if it's a little Johnny or Janie—but I'm not sure I want to know.

**JAE:** Really? You don't want to know? But if you know it's a boy or girl, you'll be able to shop for little girl things or decorate for a little boy. It would be so **convenient** to know the baby's **gender** in advance.

**LIA:** I know, I know. But I just love the idea of being surprised.

**JAE:** Well, as long as it's healthy, I guess it doesn't matter if you know in advance if it's a boy or girl.

**LIA:** Exactly! So now I will definitely start eating right. I'm going to be the perfect mom-to-be. No more fast food drive-thrus for me. Good-bye, French fries!

**JAE:** Ha, perfect! I'll get you a nice spinach salad right now—with a side of broccoli!

**TIP 1**

Most couples plan ahead for the trip to the hospital. (When a woman goes into labor, she does *not* want to stop to pack!) **Pack** a suitcase with things you'll need, and be sure to bring an address book, so you can call everyone with the news once the baby is born. And don't forget the camera!

**TIP 2**

Make sure you know the best way to the hospital! It's a good idea to drive it once or twice before the big day. You don't want to wait until the **contractions** start to try out that new GPS!

# VOCABULARY

- **accurately**: correctly
- **avoiding**: staying away from
- **birthing center**: a special place for giving birth instead of a hospital
- **Caesarean section**: a medical operation to deliver a baby when it cannot be delivered normally
- **calculate**: figure out
- **contractions**: pains that begin the birth process
- **convenient**: easy and comfortable
- **definitely**: for sure
- **delivery**: birth
- **delivery room**: the room in the hospital where childbirth happens
- **due date**: the day a baby is expected to be born
- ⓘ **eating for two**: eating and knowing that the growing baby inside is getting nutrition, too
- **expectant mothers**: pregnant women (expecting a baby)
- **forceps**: a special tool to help deliver a baby when it is not moving down the birth canal as it should
- **gender**: sex, male or female
- ⓘ **go smoothly**: happen with no problems
- ⓘ **hands-on**: helping in all the details
- **incision**: a medical cut in the body
- **labor**: the process of giving birth
- **Lamaze method**: a technique to avoid drugs for pain in childbirth
- **midwife**: a specially trained person who assists in childbirth, but who is not a doctor
- ⓘ **mom-to-be**: a pregnant woman
- **morning sickness**: feelings of nausea and sickness in the early months of pregnancy
- **nerve-racking** (can also be spelled **nerve-wracking**): very stressful
- ⓘ **new arrival**: the new baby!
- ⓘ **nowadays**: currently; in the present
- **OB/GYN**: short for *obstetrician/gynecologist*; a doctor who takes care of childbirth and women's reproductive issues
- ⓘ **the old days**: the past

- **pacing back and forth**: walking in measured steps across a room and back
- **pack**: put things you'll need into a bag or suitcase
- **pregnant**: carrying a baby inside one's body
- **prenatal**: before birth
- **recommend**: advise
- **recover**: get better; heal
- **relied on**: depended on
- ⓘ **run in the family**: be something common in a family
- **stages of labor**: the progression of the birth process
- **starting a family**: deciding to have a baby
- **surgery**: a medical operation
- ⓘ **turns out**: happens as a result of something
- **twins**: two babies born at the same time
- **ultrasound**: a special test with sound waves that can check on the baby
- **vaginal birth**: birth through the birth canal of the woman's body
- **visit**: another word for a doctor's appointment
- **vocal**: verbal; comfortable about expressing an opinion

## PRONUNCIATION POINTER

- *Obstetrician* can be a tricky word to say. That explains why so many people just say "**OB**." But it's really not that hard. It sounds like *OB–stuh–trish–in*. Go on. Say it three times fast!

- *Caesarean Section* is another scary-looking, hard-to-spell pregnancy word. This is why so many people just say, "**C-section**." Although many people *spell* it incorrectly, the pronunciation is pretty easy: *siss–AIR–ee–in SECK–shin*.

**TWINS come in twos, and so do our TWIN FUN FACTS!**

### *Fun Fact 1!*
Nigeria is famous for having lots of twins. No one is sure why there are so many twins in that country, but some people think it's because the people eat lots of yams. (Yams are similar to sweet potatoes.) Uh-oh. Yams are a favorite at Thanksgiving dinner. . . .  Be careful! Haha!

### *Fun Fact 2!*
We're not sure why, but there are lots of twin festivals. One of the most popular takes place each August in a town called, yes, *Twins*burg, Ohio.

## GRAMMAR REMINDER 1: *Will* and *Going to*

• Both *will* and *going to* take the base form of the main verb.

• Sometimes you can use either *will* or *going to*, but other times you need to be careful.

• ***Remember:*** You must use the verb *to be* before *going to*. See examples below, and note the use of contractions for the verb *to be*!

• Use ***will*** to express a future fact and when you decide to do something at the moment of speaking.
> The obstetrician **will recommend** . . . (a fact)
> I'll (**I will**) **get** you a nice spinach salad right now . . . (I decided just now)

• Use ***going to*** when something definite has been decided for the future. It can also be used when you can see that something is definitely going to happen.
> The doctor's **going to do** an ultrasound at my next visit. (already decided)
> I'm **going to be** a mom again! (It's definite. Look at my large stomach!)

# That Bundle of Joy

And you thought being pregnant was fun! Just wait until you bring home that little **bundle of joy**. Now the fun really starts. Infants can be very funny: imagine seeing your **adorable** little baby **dribbling pureed** spinach down his cute little chin! Haha!

No matter how much planning you do in advance, your life will change forever the moment you bring home your sweet little **newborn**. Suddenly, instead of **wondering** what shoes to buy at the mall, you're looking at cute, tiny baby socks for a **layette**. If you're lucky, some friends may have a **baby shower** for you. This is another time when some people set up a registry at a store so that friends will know exactly what items you need for the baby. And believe us, you'll need plenty of items! Be sure to include larger-size baby clothes on the list. Those tiny newborns grow really quickly.

Okay, let's think about this. You go into the hospital as a large mom-to-be. You come out of the hospital a little smaller, but with an entirely new person! This little person needs to be dressed when he or she leaves the hospital with you. You'll need blankets, diapers, **onesies**, socks, tee shirts, baby soap, a car seat—and that's just for the first day! Plus you'll probably need a diaper bag to tote all that stuff! The good news is that you may not have to worry about food.

One of the first decisions a new mother will make is how to feed her **infant**. Although there was a generation of babies in the United States that was **bottle-fed**, most people now believe that **breast feeding** is the healthiest choice for babies. The **nutrition** is perfect (after all, isn't that what human breasts are for?), and many doctors believe that breast milk contains **elements** that can keep the baby from getting sick. But for women who cannot, or who choose not to, breast-feed, there are many choices for infant **formula** on the market. These formulas try to be as **similar** to breast milk as possible so that babies will get the proper **nutrients**.

You may have chosen a **pediatrician** before giving birth. This is the doctor who will take care of the baby, usually until he becomes an older teenager. (Teenager already? *Aaaack!* He just arrived!) The pediatrician will answer all questions you may have about the best way to handle baby problems that may arise. One very common problem is **colic**. The baby may cry for several hours a day for no **apparent** reason. This may be because of stomach pain or fussiness.

Whatever the cause, a **fussy** baby can be very frustrating for new parents, so it's very important to take care of yourself. The more rested you are, the more **patience** you'll have when you're trying to **soothe** a crying baby. They may be cute, but babies are hard work, so you should avoid as much extra stress as you can. Does everyone want to visit so they can see the new baby? Plan certain times when this is convenient for you and when you have help. Are there **dust bunnies** under the bed? Just don't look at them! Don't worry about having a spotless house—a happy mom and baby are more important. (Of course, some very special friends may decide to get you a cleaning service. Wow! We want those friends!)

As the baby gets a little older, you'll need to be sure the house is **baby-proofed**. Once the little one starts **crawling** around, there should be nothing in his reach that can hurt him. Electrical outlets should be covered. Tables should be cleared of anything a baby can **grab**. Sharp corners should be protected. You can find plenty of tips on the Internet to help you prepare the house for your growing baby.

But the most important tip of all is this: Enjoy every minute you have with your baby! What everyone says is true: The baby years go by **in a flash**. When he's a teenager driving you crazy, you'll need all those photos and videos to remember the sweet baby days!

**TIP 3**

In the old days, new moms would carry their babies home from the hospital in their arms—even in the car. However, now every state in the country has laws requiring that babies be in a car seat *every time* they're in a car. There are different car seat types for each age and weight. Be sure to find the right one for a newborn.

**TIP 4**

(It may be Tip 4, but it's all about twos!) The **Terrible Twos!** **Toddlers** are so famous for **tantrums** and **whining** that they even have a name for it. Be sure you have a plan for staying calm when the little ones are not. Good luck!

## DIALOGUE 2: TRACK 46

**ALAN:** Wow, is that really you, Lia? I haven't seen you **in ages**! How's the baby?

**LIA:** Ha! Yeah, Alan, I don't get out much these days. I had forgotten how much work a new baby is! In fact, when Tony came home from work tonight, I told him I just had to **get out of the house** for an hour **or so**. I've been **cooped up** since the baby was born. Besides, we're almost **out of diapers**—that would be a disaster!

**ALAN:** So you're here at the supermarket for a fun **night out**! Ha, ha, ha! That's so funny! Boy, times have changed. You didn't use to go grocery shopping for an exciting night out.

**LIA:** No kidding. It seems like just yesterday that we used to go to the movies and clubs to have fun. Now fun is going to buy diapers and pureed peas.

**ALAN:** Hahahahaha! That really is funny! Yeah, I guess what they say is true: **Parenthood** will change your life.

TIP 5

*Fun* and *funny* are very tricky words for English language learners. Something that you enjoy doing is *fun*. Reading our book is *fun*. Something that makes you laugh (haha) is *funny*. Watching a baby dribble his pureed peas is *funny* (haha).

## VOCABULARY

- **adorable**: very, very cute
- **apparent**: clear
- ⓘ **baby-proofed**: made safe for a crawling baby
- **baby shower**: a party where friends give gifts that a new baby will need
- **bottle-fed**: fed milk or formula from a special baby bottle
- **breast feeding**: feeding the new baby breast milk from the mother
- ⓘ **bundle of joy**: a new baby
- **colic**: upset for a baby that may be caused by stomach pain
- **crawling**: moving around on hands and knees
- ⓘ **cooped up**: feel closed in a small space for too long
- **dribbling**: spilling from the mouth
- ⓘ **dust bunnies**: small gatherings of dust
- **elements**: ingredients
- **formula**: special milk for babies that is made to be like mother's breast milk
- **fussy**: upset; cranky; irritable
- ⓘ **get out of the house**: have a change in a boring house routine by going out
- **grab**: take and hold
- ⓘ **in a flash**: really fast

- ⓘ **in ages**: in a long time
- **infant**: a very young baby
- **layette**: the first clothes a baby needs
- **newborn**: a new baby
- **night out**: a special night doing something different or fun
- **nutrients**: things in food that the body needs
- **nutrition**: the food that the body needs
- **onesies**: special one-piece baby clothes
- ⓘ **or so**: approximately; about
- ⓘ **out of**: not having something
- **parenthood**: being a mother or father
- **patience**: ability to stay calm under stress
- **pediatrician**: a doctor who takes care of babies and children
- **pureed**: food processed in a blender until food is like a thick liquid or paste
- **similar**: like
- **soothe**: comfort
- **tantrum**: a fit of anger by an upset child
- ⓘ **Terrible Twos**: the age (around two years) when little ones are famous for being difficult
- **toddler**: a young child, just starting to walk
- **whining**: complaining with an annoying, long, questioning sound
- **wondering**: thinking about

## GRAMMAR REMINDER 2: *Used to*

When talking about something you did as a habit in the past (that you no longer do now), use *used to* plus the base form of the verb.

**Example:**
We **used to go** to the movies and clubs. (We no longer do that.)

In the negative, use **didn't** and **use to**. (No *d* on *use*!)

**Correct Example:**
You **didn't use** to go grocery shopping . . .

**Not:**
You didn't use**d** to go grocery shopping . . .

# MORE FUN WITH IDIOMATIC EXPRESSIONS:
## Babies and Parents

- **sleep like a baby**: sleep very well
  *He spent the whole day working in the garden and mowing the lawn. After all that hard work, he **slept like a baby** that night.*

- **smooth as a baby's bottom:** completely smooth; often used to talk about a man's head
  *Steven started losing his hair at age 30. By the time he was 50, his head was **smooth as a baby's bottom**.*

- **in the family way**: pregnant
  *Loretta couldn't wait to tell her friends that she was **in the family way** and would have the baby in December.*

- **pregnant pause**: stopping for a short time during a speech before saying something important
  *The teacher announced that she would give the results of the big test. After a **pregnant pause**, she said that everyone had passed.*

- **a chip off the old block**: just like a parent
  *James was **a chip off the old block**; he loved to read about archaeology, just like his father.*

 ## *Fun Fact!*

In 1914, President Woodrow Wilson signed a bill making Mother's Day a national holiday. We think he should have included a free vacation for every mother. And maybe two vacations for mothers of twins!

# Full Circle

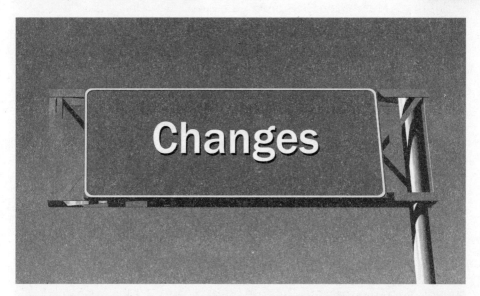

## End-of-Life Issues

Although health care in this country has made it possible for Americans to live longer and more active lives well into their **late senior years**, serious illness and death are as much a part of life as birth and living. With old age come **chronic** illnesses and serious diseases. Most of these can be treated with good medical care, but often they cannot be **cured**. When a loved one becomes ill with a serious and **incurable** disease, Americans often **rely on** the same **support systems** that they **depended on** during earlier, happier times: family and friends.

These support systems can help with important care decisions as we become sick or unable to take care of ourselves. There are many things to think about, and there are many services available to help someone facing **end-of-life issues**. Even people lucky enough to be with family may need some extra help.

As we age, many people begin to think about planning for these end-of-life issues. Family and friends can help by talking about the choices to be made. Very often a person will want to prepare a **living will** while he is still healthy.

This allows the person to make choices *now* about what care he wants to have if he becomes seriously ill. For example, some people may decide that if their heart stops, they do not want medical professionals to make it start again. This is known as a **DNR order**. The living will is a legal document that must be followed. In the living will, a person can make very clear what medical **procedures** he will allow.

A living will can be very clear about what machines someone will allow in her care plan. Someone may decide that if she is no longer able to breathe **on her own**, then she does not want to be placed on a **ventilator**. She may state in the living will that she does not want a **feeding tube**.

A person can also create a legal document called Power of Attorney that will allow another person to make all medical decisions. If someone is so sick that she cannot express herself, then the person she chooses will make decisions about health care. This person is usually a family member or a friend who knows exactly what the person's wishes are.

For someone facing the end of life, **hospice care** provides comfort and many services. A **team** of people will come to the home and make sure that the dying person is as comfortable as possible. The most important thing they hope to do is be sure the dying person has the best **quality of life** in the time he has left. The team includes doctors and nurses who will **supervise** any medical care. Because hospice care is for the dying, medical professionals are not focused on treating the illness; they are only concerned with making sure the person is comfortable and in no pain. Volunteers may help with taking care of the house and offering time off to family members who don't want to leave their loved one alone. Most health insurance plans will cover hospice care.

This isn't always an easy or happy subject to **bring up**, but it's an important one that will make things easier when a serious illness happens.

## DIALOGUE 1: TRACK 47

**LIA:** Alan, did you hear about my **great-grandmother**? You know that she's been sick for a long time now. The doctors have diagnosed **cancer**. I'm afraid the **prognosis** is not very good.

**ALAN:** Yes, I did hear the news. I'm so sorry, Lia. How is she doing?

**LIA:** Well, you know my great-grandma. *She's* doing just fine! We're all feeling a little sad about the **diagnosis**, but Granny is very **upbeat** about it.

**ALAN:** Your grandmother's mom has always been very sensible.

**LIA:** She started to **get her affairs in order** when she first got sick. And she is very clear that she doesn't want to be on machines at the end of her life. We told her, "Granny, you could let the doctors who know medicine make this decision for you." But Granny made a living will so *she* is the one deciding what kind of care she will get. Some of my aunts are a little upset. They think the doctors should do **anything and everything** to keep Granny alive, even if it means using machines to keep her lungs working.

**ALAN:** How about asking your aunts to talk to someone at the hospice center?

**LIA:** Right now they are too upset to think calmly.

**ALAN:** What about having them speak to the doctors again? Or, why don't you call the **chaplain** at the hospital? Maybe he can help with their fears.

**LIA:** That's a great idea. Maybe the chaplain can give them some comfort, so that they can see that what makes Granny comfortable is the most important thing.

 **TIP 1** Some older people enjoy giving away special **belongings** like jewelry while they are still healthy. They like to see people they love enjoy the item, and they are sure the person they want to have it will get it.

 **TIP 2** It's important to listen if someone wants to talk about plans for their death. No one wants to think about someone they love dying, but it may make the person feel better to discuss it.

## VOCABULARY

- ⓘ **anything and everything**: a strong way to say to look at all possible things to do
- • **belongings**: things a person owns
- ⓘ **bring up**: mention a subject for discussion
- • **cancer**: one of the main diseases that cause death in the United States
- • **chaplain**: a religious professional who can advise and help people in difficult times
- • **chronic**: describes something (usually a disease) that lasts for a very long time
- • **cured**: healed; made better
- ⓘ **depend on**: trust that someone will be available if needed; rely on
- • **diagnosis**: a decision about what the illness is

- **DNR order**: the short form of <u>D</u>o <u>N</u>ot <u>R</u>esuscitate; a legal order that does not allow medical attempts to make someone's heart or lungs work again
- **end-of-life issues**: things to face when death is near
- **feeding tube**: a way of giving food to someone who can't eat
- ⓘ **get one's affairs in order**: think about what needs to be done before one dies
- **great-grandmother**: *great* indicates the generation above, so a great-grandmother would be your grandmother's mother
- **hospice care**: comfort care of a person who is dying
- **incurable**: cannot be healed or made better
- **late senior years**: when a person is in the late eighties or even nineties
- **living will**: a legal statement of a person's wishes about emergency medical care
- ⓘ **on one's own**: without help from anyone
- **procedures**: processes or steps to make something happen
- **prognosis**: an opinion about what is likely to happen with a disease
- **quality of life**: a person's comfort and happiness in the time he or she has left to live
- **rely on**: trust that someone will be available if needed; depend on
- **supervise**: watch; check on
- **support system**: people who will be with you when you need them
- **team**: a group of trained people and volunteers
- ⓘ **upbeat**: feeling happy, even if there is bad news
- **ventilator**: a machine that breathes for the patient

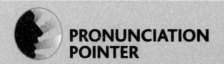

## PRONUNCIATION POINTER

There are three main ways to pronounce the /*ch*/ sound:
- *ch* as in *ch*urch
- *k* as in *k*ids (*ch*ronic)
- *sh* as in *sh*op (*ch*ef)

## GRAMMAR REMINDER 1: Making Suggestions

There are a few polite ways to make a suggestion about something. Remember we talked about using *how about* and *why don't you*?

> **How about** asking your aunts . . . ?
> **Why don't you** call the chaplain . . .?

**Here are two others:**

> **What about** having them speak to the doctors?
> Granny, **you could** let the doctors make this decision for you.

## Funeral Customs

It's the call we never want to get: In the middle of the night, the phone rings. A friend tells us that something terrible has happened. Her great-grandmother has just died. Many times this call is expected: Someone has been sick for a long time. Families who experience a **loss** become very busy **making arrangements**. Sometimes the person will have planned out a funeral in advance, but often it is the family who must make the **funeral** arrangements.

Most funerals are occasions for family and friends to meet, share memories of the person they have lost, and join in special services. **Funeral homes** will arrange to take care of the **remains**. They will prepare the **body** for a **wake**, if the family chooses. This is a common event in the United States. The body is laid in a **casket,** which is often open, for family and friends to have a final chance to say good-bye. This is known as a **viewing**. Not everyone is comfortable with this, however, and some families choose a closed **coffin**.

At a wake, the family is greeted by friends, who offer **condolences** on their loss. Close friends may arrange to send flowers to the funeral home for display, but often families will ask friends to **make a donation** to a **charity** instead. They may write in the **obituary**, "**In lieu of** flowers, please make a donation to a special charity." There are usually **visiting times** for a day or two, and then there is a funeral service, followed by **burial**. The funeral is often a church service, but it is sometimes just prayers or a speaker at the **cemetery**. If there are no religious **rites**, then the casket will be brought right to the cemetery for **interment**.

Not all families choose burial of the body in a casket, however. **Cremation** is becoming a much more common choice. Often the visiting custom is the same, but sometimes there will be no service at the cemetery. Instead, the family may have a **memorial service** several months later. Often, they will display a special **urn** with the **ashes** of their loved one. There may be a church service, or prayers, or simply a ceremony for people to talk about their memories of the person. The urn will be kept in a family member's home, or it will be buried in a cemetery. Some people will **scatter** the ashes in a favorite place. The funeral home will be able to tell you if you need special permission to do this.

During the wake period, neighbors and friends try to help in any way they can. It is common for friends to bring food to the house. This is a way to show **sympathy** for their neighbor's loss. Some families like to celebrate. This is not a party, but a way to celebrate and honor the person's life.

While this section describes the typical funeral customs, there are, of course, many different customs. Remember that the United States is made up of people with many religions and traditions, so funeral customs will also be different. For example, some people do not have a wake at all and believe it is important to bury the person within one day. Friends may visit at the home later.

All funerals are respectful of the person who has died and of the wishes of the family. Every family has special ideas about how they want to observe the death of someone they love.

## DIALOGUE 2: TRACK 48

**ALAN:** Lia, I heard that your great-grandmother **passed away**. I'm so sorry.

**LIA:** Thanks, Alan. Yes, we're all really sad about it, but we know that Granny was ready.

**ALAN:** Is there anything I can do?

**LIA:** Our neighbors have been wonderful about leaving us meals, so I don't think there's anything we need right now.

**ALAN:** Well, please accept my condolences. If you think of anything I can do to help your family, just let me know.

**LIA:** Thank you so much. If we need anything, I'll let you know.

**TIP 3**

In many parts of the country, it is customary for all cars on a road to stop for a funeral **procession**. Often, a police car will flash its lights to stop all traffic. Cars in the funeral procession have their **headlights** on to show that they are part of the funeral. When all the cars have passed by, another police car will allow the normal traffic to begin again.

Death is a part of life that sometimes makes people uncomfortable. Some people don't even like to say the word *die*. To make it easier to discuss, people use many **euphemisms**. You will probably hear the following: He's *passed*. She *passed away*. My grandmother *passed* on. All these phrases mean the same thing: Someone has died.

## VOCABULARY

- **ashes**: what is left after cremation
- **body**: what is left of the person after he or she has died
- **burial**: putting the body into the ground after the funeral
- **casket**: a special box, usually wood or metal, for the body
- **cemetery**: a place where people are buried
- **charity**: a group or organization that helps people in need
- **coffin**: another word for the casket
- **condolences**: feelings of sympathy or sadness for the friend's loss
- **cremation**: a service where the body is burned instead of buried
- **euphemism**: a way to say something that avoids words that make people uncomfortable
- **funeral**: the final service for someone who has died
- **funeral home**: a special business that takes care of funeral services and cares for the person's body
- **headlights**: the front lights of a car
- **in lieu of**: instead of (this is another French expression that we have adopted into English)
- **interment**: burial
- **loss**: what we feel when someone we love dies
- **make a donation**: give something (usually money) to a charity
- **making arrangements**: planning the funeral
- **memorial service**: a special service where friends may celebrate the person who has died
- **obituary**: a notice in the newspaper about someone's death
- ⓘ **passed, passed away, passed on**: died
- **procession**: a line of people or cars in a special ceremony
- **remains**: the body of someone who has died

- **rites**: ceremonies
- **scatter**: let go in many directions with the wind
- **sympathy**: a feeling that shows that you know someone is suffering
- **urn**: a covered container like a jar or vase for the ashes of a cremated body
- **viewing**: a time to see the body for the last time
- **visiting times**: when people may visit the family at the funeral home
- **wake**: a service where the casket is in a special room where friends and family visit

## GRAMMAR REMINDER 2: Expressions of Sympathy

These are some common ways to express sympathy when someone has died:

> **I'm so sorry** about your loss.
> You have my **sympathy.**
> You have my **condolences.**
> **Your family is in my thoughts/prayers.**

## MORE FUN WITH IDIOMATIC EXPRESSIONS: Dying

Death is one of those **taboos:** things people don't like to talk about or think about. Of course, it's always serious when someone we love dies. But when talking about death in general, lots of people find that it helps to be casual or funny about it. You may hear some of these expressions, all of which mean *to die,* even if they don't always refer to people.

- **kick the bucket**
  *He started shopping around for cars because his old one with the oil leak is about to* ***kick the bucket****.*

- **buy the farm**
  *He could tell by the third chapter of the book that the main character was going to* ***buy the farm*** *before the end.*

- **meet one's maker**
  *The cowboy in the movie told the bad guy that he was about to* ***meet his maker****.*

- **push up daisies**
  *Lots of people who talked about how safe smoking is are now* ***pushing up daisies****.*

- **bite the dust**

  *She watched as each chicken was taken from the farm to be slaughtered for dinner. Each time, she said to her brother, "Oh, well. Another one* **bites the dust***."*

### *Fun Fact!*

We bet you didn't think there could be a fun fact in this section. Well, there is. Although people don't like to say the word *die* when they're talking about death, they use the word and words related to death all the time in casual conversation: "My car died." "The battery is dead." "This play is boring me to death!"

# Review: Units 16–18

## VOCABULARY

*Fill in the blanks. Use the words below.*

| stroll | cringe | propose | elope | overdo |
|--------|--------|---------|-------|--------|
| choked | pack | soothe | crawl | dribble |

**EVA:** I really want to get married. I wish Tom would hurry up and (1)_____. He's the love of my life!

**LORETTA:** Well, why don't you go to the park for a romantic (2) _____ around the lake? Maybe he'll think that's the perfect time to ask!

**EVA:** If he does propose, maybe we'll just (3) _____, you know, run off and not tell anyone. It's so much easier than planning a big wedding.

**LORETTA:** Make sure you remember to (4) _____ your bag with everything you need before you go!

**EVA:** Can you imagine what my mom would say?

**LORETTA:** The thought of that makes me (5) _____. She'd be really upset.

**EVA:** I know. Well, at least you'd be around to (6) _____ her.

**LORETTA:** Thanks, pal! I think that would be (7) _____ing it. You know how much your family would love to see you getting hitched. They'll be all (8) _____ up seeing you in white.

**EVA:** I know, I know. They can't wait till I'm in the family way, too, but I want to put it off a while. I don't like it when babies (9)_____ all over the place when they are trying to eat.

**LORETTA:** Yes, but think how cute they are when they start to (10) _____ around on their hands and knees. Hey, don't forget I want to be the godmother!

**EVA:** I'll remember. But, hey, we still need to get Tom to hurry up and pop the question!

## INFORMAL LANGUAGE

*Match the expressions to their meanings. Try using them in a sentence.*

| | |
|---|---|
| 11. catch your eye | a. listening very carefully |
| 12. chat someone up | b. eating while pregnant |
| 13. let your hair down | c. have something common in the family |
| 14. tie the knot | d. try your hardest at something |
| 15. chip in | e. be attractive to you |
| 16. all ears | f. be sad or unhappy |
| 17. look down | g. get married |
| 18. give it your best shot | h. have a casual conversation with someone you find attractive |
| 19. eating for two | i. give money for a gift from a group of people |
| 20. run in the family | j. relax and have fun |

## GRAMMAR

*Look at the phrasal verbs in this short story. Can you explain what they mean?*

Julia first began to **(21) go out** with Jason five years ago. They always had a rocky relationship. He **(22) let her down** many times, but she always gave him another chance, and they would **(23) make up**. Finally, when she found out he was having an affair with her best friend, she decided she couldn't **(24) put up with** him any longer, and they **(25) split up** for good.

*Decide whether you need **will** or **going to** for the future tense in the following sentences. Sometimes both are possible. Remember to add the verb **to be** if you are using **going to**.*

26. Look at those huge black clouds! It _____ rain.

27. I _____ study to be a doctor this coming fall.

28. I am freezing. I think I _____ run home and get a sweater.

29. Your life _____ really change once you have a baby.

30. We _____ surprise our parents this weekend with a party because it is their wedding anniversary.

# Gadget Central

Easy Street

## Hello? Hello? Can You Hear Me Now?

WE can hear you—and we *don't* want to hear you!
  Come on, admit it. We know it's happened
to you, too. You were sitting quietly on the bus,
reading your newspaper, when she took the seat
next to you. **Yak,** yak, yak! You heard all about her
boyfriend's cooking skills. You heard about her
sister's new chocolate diet. You heard about the
neighbor's dog. Do you care? *We* don't care!

  Okay, we all love cell phones. They make it easy to
stay **in touch** with friends and family at all times. The convenient features of
smartphones are **irresistible**: hi-tech cameras, HD video, high speed Internet
access, cool **ring tones**, even GPS **guidance** to help you get where you
want to go! We remember when **voicemail, flip phones,** and **QWERTY
keyboards** for **texting were cool!** Come on, admit it. You love those **touch
screens,** games, and **applications** that can help you do just about anything
you need to do. Want to find a restaurant near your class tonight? Check your
phone. Need a map of the neighborhood? Check your phone. Want to know
what movie is showing at the theater on Tuesday? Check your phone. It may
be hard to imagine, but even the simplest early phones had keypads with a
**multi-tap function** for texting.

Oh, and if you just want to make a phone call, you can do that, too. Haha!

All of these **communication** conveniences come with a cost. And we're not just talking about the monthly bill! But now that we've mentioned it, let's talk about the monthly bill. Most companies offer a **bundle of services** for a set price each month. You can add **features** to your **plan**, but that will usually add to your bill, too. You'll have to pay for some special apps (applications) or games that you **download**. And if you want unlimited access to the Internet, you'll need to have a more expensive plan for that, too.

But the biggest cost of all this convenience is suffering when people don't **observe** simple phone **etiquette**. It's **rude** to speak loudly on the phone in a public place. It's rude when your phone rings or vibrates in a meeting. It's rude when you **interrupt** a **face-to-face** conversation to **answer** a phone call. Many places **ban** cell phone use. Some trains have special "quiet cars" where no cell phones are allowed. Good cell phone etiquette means that you are respectful of others around you. No matter how interesting your **bowl of cereal** is to you, trust us: The guy sitting next to you does not want to hear about it!

## DIALOGUE 1: TRACK 49

**ALAN:** Good morning, Officer. Was I speeding when you pulled me over? I thought I was being very careful.

**POLICE OFFICER:** I didn't pull you over for speeding. I pulled you over because you were talking on a cell phone while driving.

**ALAN:** For talking on the phone? Is that a problem? My wife just called to remind me about an appointment when I get back from my business trip.

**POLICE OFFICER:** Sir, using a **handheld device** while driving is **illegal** in this state.

I can see from your **plates** that you're from out of town, so I'll **let you go** with just a warning this time. But, sir, next time just check the law before your trip. Maybe you should buy a hands-free device if you do a lot of driving for business.

**ALAN:** I will do that, Officer. In fact, I was thinking about buying a **Bluetooth earpiece** when I bought my phone. I will **definitely** get one as soon as I get home. Thanks.

**POLICE OFFICER:** By the way, I hope you weren't texting when I pulled you over. Texting while driving is even more dangerous than talking.

## VOCABULARY

- **answer**: take the phone call
- **application**: a game or tool that you can download to your phone; things your phone can do
- **ban**: not allow; forbid
- **Bluetooth**: the special system that lets electronic devices work without wires or hands
- **bowl of cereal**: a typical American breakfast made of dried grains like wheat and oats
- **bundle of services**: a group of things your phone can do
- **communication**: giving and getting information; for example, TV, radio, telephone, computer
- **definitely**: for sure; absolutely
- **download**: take from the Internet so that you can use it on your phone
- **earpiece**: part of a phone that you can wear so you don't have to use your hands to hold the phone and talk
- **etiquette**: ways to be polite
- **face-to-face**: in person; with the person right there
- **features**: special things something can do
- **flip phone**: phone that folds
- **function**: use
- **guidance**: help
- **handheld device**: a phone or other device that needs hands to operate
- **illegal**: against the law
- **interrupt**: stop something while it's going on
- ⓘ **in touch**: connected by talking
- **irresistible**: so great you *have* to have it!

- ⓘ **let someone (or something) go**: not hold someone responsible for something; ignore something (to let someone *off the hook)*
- **multi-tap**: selecting a letter on a phone by tapping the number key that corresponds to that letter
- **observe**: obey; use
- **plan**: the services you select for a certain price per month
- **plates** (also **tags**): license plates on a car
- **QWERTY keyboard**: letters arranged as on a typical English computer keyboard (look at the top row of letters!)
- **ring tone**: the sound your phone makes to let you know someone is calling
- **rude**: not polite
- **texting**: sending typed messages by cell phone
- **touch screen**: instead of typing, just touch to select an option
- **voicemail**: system of keeping recorded messages when you can't answer a call
- ⓘ **yak**: have a very casual conversation (usually about nothing!)

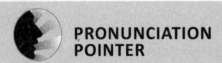

## PRONUNCIATION POINTER

*Cell* and *sell* are both pronounced the same way. The fancy word we use to talk about these words is *homophones*. Homophones are words that sound the same but are spelled differently.

## GRAMMAR REMINDER 1: The Past Continuous Tense with the Past Simple Tense

The past continuous tense is often used with the simple past tense to show one longer action that was interrupted by a shorter action.

**For example:**
> He **was speeding** when the police officer **stopped** him.
> *Was speeding* is the long action; *stopped* is the action that interrupts the longer action.

Remember books? We remember books. The paper kind. With pages. (Hey, you're reading one now! Unless you have the e-book, haha.) In the **good old days** before computers, people read printed books and newspapers to get information. Students spent hours and hours in the library, looking for information in **dusty** old books for class assignments. **Essays** were **handwritten**; if students made a mistake, they would **toss** the paper and start writing all over again. Now? Information is **instant**! Students can find anything on the Internet in minutes and then **compose** a **document** on their **laptops**, all while sitting on the sofa. If they make a mistake, they can just **delete** or **cut, copy,** and **paste** to move bits of text around. Maybe the most important computer skill is knowing how to **back up** your files in case your computer **crashes**, or you drop your device in the lake. Documents and files can be sent to "the cloud" for storage. We're not really sure what "the cloud" is, but we know it makes it easy to find stuff from any device! Ha, we remember when all we got from clouds was rain! We still like to keep another backup file, just to be doubly-sure that our hard work won't be lost forever in **cyberspace**.

We also remember the library in the good old days. It was a place where everyone was quiet. **Hum** along to an iPod **tune**? Never! Send an **e-mail** while working? What's e-mail? Watch a movie on the **HDTV** while you work? Impossible! Download **MP3s** to your **hard drive** or **device**? No! But now students can watch **YouTube** videos about their **research** topic as they write a paper. And as they are writing, they can **IM** friends in another **window** on their computer **screen**. A simple **click** of the **mouse, hit SAVE,** and students can take a quick chat break. Wait. Did you think we were talking about chatting with someone in the same room? No! We're talking about **online** chat rooms. You don't even need to **hook up** a **webcam**; just open an app and it's party time instead of homework time!

Do we sound like **dinosaurs**? Actually, we love technology. With social networking apps, and **cable** and **satellite signals**, electronic devices and HDTVs can **broadcast** important local information instantly. In areas where **severe** weather is a problem, TV is an excellent **source** of **warning**s. Your local radio or TV station can give information about where to get help or what to do to keep your family and home safe. Hurricane updates can help you prepare your house. If a tornado is coming, you can get to a safe area. If there's a **snowstorm**, people often turn to radio or TV to hear about school closings. School is closing? Yay! Quick—text your buddy the good news!

Technology is our friend! Instant communication is convenient, fun, and easy. But for those of us who still like to hold a piece of paper with the words of friends, there is always **snail mail**.

## Fun Fact!

It's the latest thing: cell-phone **sniffing** dogs! Yes, many American prisons are using specially trained dogs that can smell and find any part of a cell phone that a prisoner may have hidden.

## DIALOGUE 2: TRACK 50

**ALAN:** Uh-oh.

**LIA:** That sounds like trouble. What happened?

**ALAN:** I was answering an e-mail, and I hit *Reply All.*

**LIA:** So, what's the problem?

**ALAN:** Well, the problem is that my e-mail reply said, "I don't want to go to this meeting! I want to go to lunch!"

**LIA:** *Aaackkk!* Were you thinking that the e-mail would just go to your friend?

**ALAN:** Yes! I wasn't reading the other names on the list, so I didn't see that the boss was also on the list!

**LIA:** Well, you really need to be careful about sending e-mail. Once you hit *Send*, it's gone. You can't get it back.

**ALAN:** I know. And even if the e-mail comes from a friend, I have to remember that there are other people on the list, too. The boss sent me a reply: "Is it your lunchtime, Alan?"

**LIA:** Well, I don't think you'll get fired over an e-mail that says you want to go to lunch, but maybe you should explain to your boss that you were only kidding. It was just a little joke about going to lunch instead of going to the meeting. Was he wondering why you were so hungry?

**ALAN:** No. He wasn't wondering why I was hungry. I think he was wondering why he hired me in the first place!

Before you reply to an e-mail, be sure to check if you are hitting **Reply** or **Reply All**. *Reply All* means your note will be seen by every person on the list. This could be embarrassing if you write something you don't want your boss to see and his or her name is on the list!

## VOCABULARY

- **acronym**: a word formed by the first letters of a phrase (see list on page 210)
- **broadcast**: air (send) information over TV or radio signals
- **cable**: a way to receive TV service through fiber-optic wires
- **compose**: write
- ⓘ **dinosaur**: ancient creatures that lived on earth millions of years ago; used to describe people who don't use new technology
- **dusty**: with a light covering of dirt
- **essay**: a piece of writing about a single topic
- ⓘ **good old days**: how things were when you were younger
- **handwritten**: written with a pen or pencil on paper!
- **HDTV**: short for <u>H</u>igh <u>D</u>efinition <u>Tele</u><u>V</u>ision; yields a very clear TV picture on the screen
- **hook up**: connect
- **hum**: sing a song without the words
- **instant**: right away! this second! no waiting!
- **research**: careful study about a topic
- **satellite**: a way to receive TV service from satellites in space
- **severe**: very harsh
- **signal**: a message carried by light waves that lets electronic devices communicate (Don't ask us—it's science-y!)
- ⓘ **snail mail**: the postal service
- ⓘ **sniffing**: smelling
- **snowstorm** (also **blizzard**): lots of snow
- **source**: a place to get information
- **toss**: throw in the trash
- **tune**: a musical song or melody
- **warning**: advance notice about something
- **YouTube**: a website with videos about everything

They look exactly the same! They are spelled exactly the same way. But the present tense and the past tense of the verb *read* are pronounced very differently.

The present tense is pronounced **reed**.
The past tense is pronounced **red**.

## GRAMMAR REMINDER 2: The Past Continuous Tense—Affirmative Statements, Negatives

The past continuous tense is used to talk about a long continuing action in the past.

Form it by using the past tense of the verb *to be* and the *-ing* form of the verb. To form the negative, simply add *not* or *-n't* after the verb *to be*.

Take a look at these examples from the readings and dialogues in this unit:

**Positive:**
You **were** sitt**ing** quietly on the bus.
I thought I **was** be**ing** very careful.

**Negative**:
I hope you **weren't** text**ing**. *(were not)*
I **wasn't** read**ing** the other names on the list. *(was not)*
He **wasn't** wonder**ing** why I was hungry. *(was not)*

## GRAMMAR REMINDER 3: The Past Continuous Tense—Questions

To form a question using the past continuous tense, just put the form of the verb *to be* first, then the subject, and finally the *-ing* form of the verb.

Take a look at these examples from the readings and dialogues in this unit:

**Was** I speed**ing**?
**Were** you think**ing** that the e-mail would just go to your friend?
**Was** he wondering why you were so hungry?
Remember to add a question word at the beginning as you need it, e.g., "***What*** were you thinking?"

# COMPUTER WORDS

**back up**: save your files in another place in case the computer stops working

**click**: the word we use to mean press the **key** (computer mouse button)

**copy**: the computer choice that lets you copy something you want to move

**crash**: when the computer stops working and you can't open your files

**cut**: the computer choice that lets you remove something from a document

**cyberspace**: where computers all communicate (It's a mystery to us ☺.)

**delete**: erase something you've written

**desktop**: a large computer that sits on a desk and does not move easily

**document**: something written on the computer

**e-mail**: electronic mail; notes you send from your computer

**hard drive**: the important part of the computer with all the parts that make it work

**hit**: a casual word meaning *click*

**IM**: Instant Message (If you write to a person who is online, they can answer instantly.)

**laptop**: a small computer that you can carry and use on your lap

**mouse**: a small device to make the computer do what you want (not a rodent!)

**MP3**: a file that lets you put music on your computer or iPod

**online**: connected to the Internet

**paste**: the computer choice that lets you move something you copied

**Reply**: what you click to answer e-mail; sends *only* to the person who sent the message

**Reply All**: what you click to answer e-mail if you want everyone on the list to get your message

**save**: the computer choice that keeps whatever you're working on in a file

**screen**: the part of the computer that you look at; on a desktop it's called the **monitor**

**webcam**: the camera that you connect to your computer

**window**: what you see on your screen when you open the computer

# TEXT TALK!

It may seem like a whole new language, but using **acronyms** while texting or chatting can really save time. And because they're used as shortcuts, people often don't bother with capital letters.

Just make sure you keep these to text talk. A boss does *not* want to see these in reports!

**ASAP**: as soon as possible
**b/c**: because
**bf**: boyfriend
**gf**: girlfriend
**bff**: best friends forever
**btw**: by the way
**FAQ**: frequently asked questions
**FYI**: for your information
**GL**: good luck
**gtg** or **gg**: gotta go
**j/k**: just kidding

**K**: okay
**L8R**: later (see you later)
**LOL**: laughing out loud
**ROFL**: rolling on the floor laughing
**thx**: thanks
**ttyl**: talk to you later
**txt**: text
**ty**: thank you
**ur**: your
**VM**: voice mail
**xoxo**: hugs and kisses

## MORE FUN WITH IDIOMATIC EXPRESSIONS: Technology

- **bells and whistles**: extra features to make something even more special
  *Jane bought a new cell phone with all the **bells and whistles**. She can play games, access the Internet, and even make phone calls!*

- **cutting edge**: very new technology
  *My computer is **cutting edge**. It can recognize my voice from the next room!*

- **computer geek**: someone who knows about computers and spends lots of time with them
  *My nephew is a real **computer geek**. He spends hours every day just finding new things to do with his computer.*

- **dead zone**: an area where your cell phone won't work
  *I need to find a new company for my cell phone. My house is in a **dead zone** for the one I have.*

- **waste of minutes**: not worth talking to; not worth using your cell-phone plan minutes
  *He never has anything interesting to say. It's yak, yak, yak about nothing. Talking to him is a **waste of minutes**.*

# 9 to 5

## The Perfect Job

Are you **fed up** with **getting paid peanuts**? Do you feel that your boss is always **picking on** you? Is it starting to **get you down**? Uh-oh. We can feel it—you want to **quit**! Well, that's okay, but be sure you don't just **walk out** one day. Think about it carefully. Make sure you have **all your ducks in a row** before you go. Even if you think you may have another job **lined up**, don't **put all your eggs in one basket**. Nothing is official until you've **signed on the dotted line**, so make sure you have all the paperwork for the new job before you **hand in your notice** at the old one.

Of course, we don't always have a choice about finding a new job. Maybe you've been **let go,** or your company has **gone under.** Either way, it's time to start looking for a new job and **make a fresh start.**

The thought of finding a new job can be overwhelming, and you may be wondering where to start. There are plenty of options. Maybe the most important thing is to think about what you're good at. Can you **capitalize on** that? Maybe it's time to think about learning new **skills**. How is your English? Good language skills usually improve your chances for a better-paying job. So how can you do this? The good news is that reading this book is a great **first step** ☺.

Taking an ESL class is another great way to improve. English classes are usually lots of fun, and you'll meet new people from all over the **globe**. Why not sign up with a friend and make it a fun night out? Some classes are free, like those sponsored by churches and libraries; others you may need to pay for. Community colleges and adult education centers are usually the most **affordable**. Some schools even offer very specialized English classes for different professions. But don't forget about the skills that you already have. You speak another language; maybe you can teach that to someone else. Think of it: you could set up a language exchange with an American where part of the time you talk in English and the other part you speak in your language. This is a great way to meet new friends. And don't forget that many companies look for people who can speak another language.

If you want to learn a **trade,** think about technical colleges and community colleges. There are schools that specialize in certain areas. For example, if you want to learn about working in the computer industry, there are schools that teach only computer technology. If you've always wanted to work in the dental field, you can go to a school that teaches only what you need to know about dentistry. Haha. We wonder if they teach a class about how to say, "Open wide!"

Okay, so where can you find this new job? There is no magic answer for how to find the perfect job. Many people rely on **word of mouth**. A friend tells you that her company is looking for a new person. Or you can look in the **classifieds** of your local paper, which posts its listings online these days. Many towns and community centers have career centers with lots of information about local companies that have jobs. And, of course, the Internet offers lots of options if you use it well. Type in the name of the company you're interested in. Then click the **Human Resources** link and search the **current** openings. You can even fill out the **application** online. You might want to look online at **headhunters** and **employment agencies**, too. You can **plug in** the type of job you are looking for, and they will send you **periodic updates** and **listings**. Many places will ask for references. References are people who know you and your work and will tell a potential employer that you're a good worker. If you want to use someone as a **reference,** be sure to ask him before **submitting** his name. If you want people to say good things about you, it helps if they are expecting the question before the new employer calls.

Okay, so you've found a job you think is your dream job. It's really important to **look beyond** the salary they will be paying you. It's important to be sure you're a **good fit** for the job. And it's important to think about the entire **compensation package**. What **benefits** does the company offer?

The one most people check out first is a health plan. These plans can be very complex and confusing, so **do your homework** and make sure you understand what is **included** and what is **excluded**. You may get a choice of different plans, and the company will probably give you paperwork explaining each. If you have questions, the person with all the benefits information is the **HR** specialist. Other benefits may include dental insurance, life insurance, and **short-term** and **long-term disability** insurance. You can **elect** or **decline** some of these; if you elect to take them, you will probably have to pay some amount out of each paycheck for the extra coverage. Think carefully. If you choose not to take the insurance and something happens, you could be **looking at** a huge bill. Other things to think about when you get a job offer are **vacation time** and **sick leave**. How many days will you get? Does the company offer a **pension plan**? Some places will even offer **tuition reimbursement**. It's all pretty complicated, but it's really important stuff. It takes a lot of work to find the dream job!

## DIALOGUE 1: TRACK 51

**LIA:** Hey, Alan, look at you reading the newspaper! But **how come** you're reading the classifieds? Don't you usually prefer the comics? Haha.

**ALAN:** Very funny. And anyway, I already finished reading the comics. Now I'm looking for a new job.

**LIA:** No kidding? Uh-oh. Is there a problem at work?

**ALAN:** I guess you could say that. I've worked at that fast food **joint** for two years now doing the **same old stuff**, and it's time for a change. Besides, I've eaten **way too many** of their burgers, and I can't fit into any of my pants!

**LIA:** Well, I can understand wanting to make a change. And after all, you speak two languages **fluently**. There are plenty of companies that have great jobs for people who are **bilingual**. Not too many Americans speak two languages. With world economies so connected, companies need to have people who can communicate in another language, as well as English.

**ALAN:** That's exactly what I think. I know it's a big **plus** to be bilingual these days. And I think if I can find a job with a better salary, I'll be able to buy that new car I really want.

**LIA:** Yeah, and if you have that new car, maybe you'll finally be able to **convince** Margaret to go out with you!

**ALAN:** Exactly! I've had a **crush** on her for **ages**!

The holiday season is a good time to find a **part-time** job. Many people are shopping for holiday gifts, and stores often hire extra people.

TIP 2

Your chances of finding part-time work are even better if you can do **shift work**. Often stores need extra people to work when the store is closed to arrange **merchandise** on shelves.

## VOCABULARY

- **affordable**: not too expensive
- ⓘ **ages**: a long time
- ⓘ **all your ducks in a row**: have a plan
- **application**: an information form that you need to fill out to get a job
- **benefits**: special things you get on your job in addition to pay
- **bilingual**: knowing two languages fluently
- **capitalize on**: take advantage of
- **classifieds**: ads for jobs
- **compensation package**: the salary and benefits of a job
- **convince**: persuade; make someone think something
- ⓘ **crush**: feeling that you really like someone (romantically)
- **current**: now
- **decline**: refuse; not take
- ⓘ **do your homework**: do research to find out about something
- **elect**: choose
- **excluded**: not part of something
- ⓘ **fed up**: tired of something
- **first step**: starting to take action
- **fluently**: very well
- ⓘ **getting paid peanuts**: getting very little pay
- ⓘ **get you down**: make you feel discouraged
- **globe**: the world
- ⓘ **gone under**: failed
- ⓘ **good fit**: a good match for your interests and skills

- **hand in your notice**: tell your boss that you will be leaving your job after a certain time period
- **headhunters, employment agencies**: companies that work to find people jobs
- ⓘ **how come**: why
- **Human Resources** (also called **HR**): the department that takes care of employees
- **included**: part of something
- ⓘ **joint**: place
- ⓘ **let go**: lose your job
- ⓘ **lined up**: have things planned in order
- **listings**: notices about job openings
- **long-term disability**: being unable to work for a long time because of sickness or injury
- **look beyond**: think about more than just one thing
- ⓘ **looking at**: expecting to happen
- **make a fresh start**: start again
- **merchandise**: things for sale
- **9 to 5**: a job (usual job hours are 9 a.m. to 5 p.m.)
- **part-time**: working just a few hours of a day
- **pension plan**: a system that saves money so that you can collect small payments when you are no longer working
- **periodic**: occurring at different intervals
- ⓘ **picking on**: always watching and criticizing or always giving work to someone
- ⓘ **plug in**: enter into a form
- ⓘ **plus**: advantage
- ⓘ **put all your eggs in one basket**: depend on one thing happening (which may not happen!)
- ⓘ **quit**: leave your job
- **reference**: someone who will give you a good recommendation
- ⓘ **same old stuff** (also **same old, same old**): the same routine; every day is the same thing
- **shift work**: unusual work hours, not 9 to 5; perhaps working overnight
- **short-term disability**: being unable to work because of sickness or injury for a short time
- **sick leave**: days off when you are sick that you will get paid for

- ⓘ **signed on the dotted line**: signed a contract
- **skills**: talents or abilities
- **submit**: give
- **trade**: a job that needs special skills
- **tuition reimbursement**: money back for what you have spent on education
- **updates:** new information, or changes to a product
- **vacation time**: days off that you will get paid for
- ⓘ **walk out**: leave your job without letting your supervisor know in advance
- ⓘ **way too many/much**: a stronger way of saying very many/much
- ⓘ **word of mouth**: hearing something from another person

## GRAMMAR REMINDER 1: The Present Perfect Simple Tense— Affirmative Statements

The present perfect simple tense can be used to show something that started in the past and has not yet finished. It's formed by the verb *to have* and the past participle. What's a *past participle,* you say? For regular verbs, it's the same as the past simple: just add *–ed*. For the irregular verbs, you just have to memorize the form. (See the list of irregular verbs in Appendix B.)

Take a look at these examples with the regular verb *to work*:
    I **have** (I**'ve**) work**ed** here for two years now.
    He **has** (he**'s**) work**ed** here for two years.
    They started working here in the past, and they are still working here now.

Take a look at this example from the dialogue using the irregular verb *to have*:
    I**'ve had** a crush on her for ages.
    I had a crush on her in the past, and I still have a crush on her now.

*Note:* In spoken English, we usually use the contractions **I've** worked, **he's** worked, and so on.

## GRAMMAR REMINDER 2: The First Conditional

The first conditional is used to show the *probable* result of a *possible* action. It can be written in two ways:
    If I get a new job, **I will** (I**'ll**) have more money.
    I**'ll have** more money if I get a new job.

Having more money is the *probable* result. Getting a new job is the *possible* action.

**Note:** Don't mix *if* and *will* in the same clause!
Do *not* say: If **I will get** a new job, I have a new car.

## PRONUNCIATION POINTER

*I'll* is pronounced *eye-l*.
It's not pronounced *ill*, as in "I'm sick; I need to go to the doctor!"

## Paperwork!

*Ack!* We all hate paperwork! It takes ages to do, but there's no getting away from the fact that you will probably need lots of papers for your job search. You'll need to write a **résumé** and a **cover letter**, and you'll probably need **transcripts** for the education you have completed. These documents are summaries of your experience. The cover letter is a formal letter of interest in the job, explaining why you would be an excellent fit for the company, and how your past **accomplishments** will help the company. The résumé shows all the work you've done. The transcript shows all the classes you've taken. If all your education was received outside the United States, you may want to consider hiring a company that can **Americanize** your transcript; that is, it will analyze your courses to see how they match up to similar courses in the United States, and they will figure out your **GPA**.

Although some companies still hire new employees using only a paper or online application **form** (without requiring a résumé), for many jobs, you will probably need to complete both. We know, we know. It seems like a **waste of time,** but hey, **gotta** keep the **big wigs** happy! No matter what paperwork you need for a new job, it's a good idea to think through all your previous experience and skills before an **interview**. You'll need to be **on the ball** to really **sell yourself**. The interview is a very short time to give as much information as you can.

Writing a good cover letter and résumé is an **art form**! There are hundreds of books and articles about how to do this, and, of course, there's a ton of free information online. It's important to choose information that applies to the type of position you are looking for. Although it may take a lot of time, it really is **worth** doing this well. Make sure you get someone to check it over for you. Employers say that there is nothing worse than looking at a résumé full of **errors**. (Hoo boy, we know. We've seen some **beauts**!) If an employer thinks that you didn't put much effort into your paperwork, he may think that you'll be the type of employee who doesn't put much effort into his job. Employers often go by **first appearances**, so it's a great idea to have an **extra pair of eyes** to **look over** your writing.

Before a new employer even meets you, he may make judgments about you based on your résumé and cover letter. And once you've prepared a good résumé (and you've saved a copy to your computer and backed it up!), all you'll need to do is **tweak** it as your skills and work experience grow. This paperwork could mean the difference between getting your dream job or not.

## PRONUNCIATION POINTER

*Beaut* is pronounced *byute*. It's like *beauty*: *byut ee*. Beautiful!

**TIP 3** You can find a ton of **templates** for cover letters and résumés online. Don't forget your local library! Libraries have plenty of job search help!

### Fun Fact!
We can all use an extra pair of eyes to look over important paperwork. Even the president has people to help look over his speeches.

### DIALOGUE 2: TRACK 52

**ALAN:** Hey, Lia, I could use an extra pair of eyes. Would you mind looking this over for me?

**LIA:** Sure. What is it?

**ALAN:** My résumé. Instead of looking for something new, I've decided to apply to be a **supervisor** at the place where I work now, and I really want to make a good impression.

**LIA:** Wow, and I can see you spent a lot of time preparing this résumé.

**ALAN:** Yeah, I've thought about that supervisor job all weekend, and I decided I just have to **give it a shot.**

**LIA:** Good for you! You have some great experience, and you'll be a perfect fit for that position.

**ALAN:** That's what I was thinking, too. Some of the things I've already accomplished in my job show that I can really handle the extra **responsibilities.** I think if I just get an interview with the boss, I'll be able to sell myself. And if I get the job, I'll be **thrilled.** It's exactly what I've been looking for.

**LIA:** I'm sure they'll want a reference. Have you thought about whom you're going to ask?

**ALAN:** Yes. My supervisor now has already said he'll give me a great reference. And just to be sure I get plenty of support, I've also called Mrs. Robinson from the James Rinski Company. That's the company where I used to work when I first arrived in the United States. She was my supervisor.

**LIA:** Great idea! I remember that she really liked you and thought you were one of the best workers on her team. But I don't remember why you left that job. What happened?

**ALAN:** The company had to **downsize,** and there was a big **layoff**. I was in the last group that they laid off. They **eliminated** my position. I know Mrs. Robinson **felt really bad** when she had to let me go. She said she would be happy to help me any way she could with finding a new job.

**LIA:** Sounds like she'll be a perfect reference. I'm sure she'll be really happy to give you a great **recommendation**. Good luck!

**ALAN:** Thanks. I'll need luck—and a résumé with no mistakes!

### *Fun Fact!*
Many workplaces have "dress down Friday" when you can wear casual clothes. Take our advice: find out what the policy is! If you're the only one wearing a suit, you will feel silly. If you're the only one wearing jeans, you will feel **ridiculous**! (We know—we've been there.)

# VOCABULARY

- **accomplishments**: good things you've done at work
- ⓘ **Americanize**: make something seem similar to the way it looks in the U.S.
- ⓘ **art form**: making something perfect and special
- ⓘ **beautiful**: great! fantastic!
- ⓘ **beauts**: amazing examples!
- ⓘ **big wigs**: executives or other important people in a company
- **cover letter**: a letter expressing interest in a job
- **downsize**: make a company smaller by laying off people
- **eliminated**: ended; got rid of
- **errors**: mistakes
- ⓘ **extra pair of eyes**: a person who can help find mistakes or make suggestions
- ⓘ **felt bad**: felt sad about something
- **first appearances**: how things seem right away, before getting to know someone
- **form**: a document to be completed with your information
- ⓘ **give it a shot**: give something a try
- ⓘ **gotta**: very casual way of saying *have to*
- **GPA**: short for **G**rade **P**oint **A**verage; your overall grade in school
- **interview**: a meeting between someone who wants the job and the person who is hiring
- **layoff**: ending the employment of some people, usually because there is not enough work
- ⓘ **look over**: check; read for mistakes
- ⓘ **on the ball**: alert; prepared
- **recommendation**: a good reference, a good report about your work
- **responsibilities**: jobs or tasks that someone is in charge of doing well
- **résumé**: a summary of your work experience
- **ridiculous**: very silly
- ⓘ **sell yourself**: be able to explain why you are such an excellent person for the job
- **supervisor**: a person in a leadership position at work; a manager or boss
- **template**: an easy design to use for making a document
- **thrilled**: really happy and excited

- **transcript**: a summary of courses you have studied
- **tweak**: make small changes to add or change information
- ⓘ **waste of time**: something that is not worth doing
- **worth**: of value

## MORE FUN WITH IDIOMATIC EXPRESSIONS: Jobs

- **dead-end job**: a job that offers no chance for improvement
  *There's no chance of a promotion in the office where I work. It's really a dead-end job.*

- **crack the whip**: make people work really hard
  *That new boss of mine is really cracking the whip in the office. We don't get a minute to chat.*

- **work your fingers to the bone**: work really hard
  *I really hope the boss appreciates the work I've done on this project. I've worked my fingers to the bone to make it perfect.*

- **call it quits**: end something
  *It's no good. I'm fed up with my job. I've decided to call it quits and look for something new.*

- **learn the ropes**: learn how to do something; get used to doing a new job
  *My new job is a bit stressful, but I'm sure it will be easier once I learn the ropes.*

## GRAMMAR REMINDER 3: More Present Perfect Simple Tense

The present perfect simple tense is another tense that works really hard. It can also be used to show a recent action:

> **I've decided** to apply to be a supervisor.

# USAGE REMINDER

Looking for a job is one of those times when it's important to remember when to use **formal** English and when to use **informal** English.

Wow, this is a huge topic, but here are some general tips:

| Okay in Informal English | Use This in Formal English |
| --- | --- |
| **Contractions** | **Full form** |
| **I've worked** there for five years. | **I have worked** there for five years. |
| **Phrasal verbs** | **Full form** |
| The company **laid me off** when they lost a major customer. | The company **eliminated my position** when they lost a major customer. |
| **Idiomatic expressions** | **Literal language** |
| **I worked my fingers to the bone** for my company. | **I worked very hard** for my company. |
| **Informal vocabulary** | **More formal vocabulary** |
| I worked with an **awesome bunch of guys**. | I worked with a **wonderful group of people**. |
| **Incomplete sentences** | **Complete sentences** |
| Great idea! | That's a great idea. |

# The Big Interview

Dream Job

## Before . . .

Well done! To **land** an interview is a big accomplishment. Your first **reaction** will probably be excited relief. Then comes the next thought: "I don't want to **blow it**! How can I make sure I **nail** the interview?" You made a good impression with your application; now you need to **follow up** with a great personal impression.

You've got to prepare. One great **strategy** is to practice with a **mock** interview. Before the big day, ask someone **in the know** to help. Some people even make a video of themselves in a practice interview so they can see how they **come across** when they answer questions. Think about the questions your interviewer is most likely to ask. Practice your answers, but be careful to sound natural and not to sound too **staged**.

It's possible that they'll throw you a curveball and ask a question you never expected. Just stay calm and answer the best you can. Do your homework! Make sure you know about the company and the job responsibilities. Interviewers often ask why you want to work for them. Make sure you have an answer that shows you know about the company.

It's **natural** to be nervous, but it's important to look **confident**. You'll feel more confident if you look professional and feel comfortable. Choose clothes that are **conservative**. Save the tee shirt and jeans for when you get home and need to **unwind**!

Finally, before you go, make sure you know exactly where the interview is. Sometimes we *think* we know where something is, but the exact street address can be tricky to find. You do *not* want to get lost or have to walk very far before your interview. Allow plenty of time to arrive early so you can relax a bit. *Never* be late! It's important to make a good **first impression**. Trust us. An interviewer will not be impressed by someone who can't be **on time**.

## DIALOGUE 1: TRACK 53

**ALAN:** Hey, guess what? I got the call.

**LIA:** The call? What are you talking about? What call?

**ALAN:** I got a call about that job I wanted! Remember? You helped me with my résumé. It's the supervisor position, and I've got an interview tomorrow! Wow, if I get this, it'll be a real **feather in my cap.** I'm pretty excited.

**LIA:** That's awesome, Alan. And you've worked there for **quite a while**, so you've already got your **foot in the door**. Where's the interview?

**ALAN:** It's at the **head office**.

**LIA:** Oh boy. **Where on earth** is that?

**ALAN:** Oh, it's somewhere down Industrial Road. I have the address written down somewhere. I have a pretty good idea of where the office is.

**LIA:** A pretty good idea? You'd better make sure you know *exactly* where it is. Industrial Road is pretty long, and there are a lot of **cul-de-sacs**. Whatever you do, you can't be late! You have only one chance to make a good first impression, and you'll blow it if the interviewer has to wait for you. Being late will not help you nail the job.

**ALAN:** Yeah, I thought of that. I think I'll drive down to the office tonight and check it out. I'll be more confident in the morning if I know exactly where I'm going, and how long it will take to get there.

**LIA:** Good plan. Don't forget to leave extra time for traffic in the morning. Have you decided what you're going to wear?

**ALAN:** I think the company is pretty casual, so I thought I might wear my new jeans. And I bought a new pair of sneakers last week. What do you think?

**LIA:** *Aacckk!* No way! If this is a supervisor job, you may need to dress a bit more upscale. Even if jeans are okay on the job, I think you should wear some other pants to the interview. I think you should even wear a **suit jacket** if you have one. And how about a tie? Even if it's a casual place, you will look very professional to the interviewer.

**ALAN:** Okay, okay. So, I guess that means no sneakers, too. Well, the good news is that if I don't get this job, maybe I can get a job as a fashion model.

**LIA:** Haha. Well then at least you won't have to worry about clothes.

**TIP 1**

Yes, you need to think about how to dress for an interview, but just as important is to think about what you *eat* before the interview. You'll be sitting pretty close to the hiring manager, so you may want to think carefully before you have onions and garlic for lunch! Also, spinach in your teeth is not a good look for anyone. Be sure to check the mirror before you go out!

## VOCABULARY

- ⓘ **blow it**: ruin your chance to do something
- ⓘ **come across**: seem to someone
- • **confident**: sure of yourself
- • **conservative**: traditional
- • **cul-de-sac**: a short street that is closed at one end
- ⓘ **feather in one's cap**: an accomplishment to be proud of
- • **first impression**: how you seem to someone when he or she first meets you
- ⓘ **follow-up**: continue with something you started
- ⓘ **foot in the door**: first step in working toward a goal
- • **head office**: the main office of a company
- ⓘ **in the know**: an expert at something
- ⓘ **land**: get something you've tried for
- • **mock**: practice
- ⓘ **nail**: do something perfectly
- • **natural**: normal
- • **on time**: arrive when you're supposed to be there, not late!
- ⓘ **quite a while**: a pretty long time
- • **reaction**: response

- **staged**: looking too practiced or memorized
- **strategy**: plan
- **suit jacket**: a business-style jacket to wear with pants
- **unwind**: relax
- ⓘ **where on earth**: a stronger way of saying *where*

*Usage reminder: Pretty* can mean beautiful, but it's also an informal way of saying *quite* or *rather.*

**For example:**
**Pretty** *excited* is the same as **quite** *excited.*
**Pretty** *casual* is the same as **rather** *casual.*

## PRONUNCIATION POINTER

**Practice:** In spoken English, *going to* sounds like **gonna.** (**What are you gonna wear?**)

Got to (**must**) sounds like **gotta.** (You've **gotta** prepare.)

### *Fun Fact!*
During a job interview, an interviewer asked if the candidate would like some coffee. The candidate said, "That sounds great! Do you mind if I eat my doughnut with that?"
Um . . . he did *not* get the job.

# During . . .

You made it on time and you look great! The interviewer brings you into a room and, *wham!* There's an entire **panel** waiting to interview you. You may have expected to speak with just one person, but sometimes a company likes to have an entire group of people ask questions. Wow. It may be **intimidating,** but don't let this **throw you**. You are well prepared, you've done your research, and you've done a **dry run**. You're ready!

Actually, the interview begins as soon as you meet your interviewer. It's usually customary to shake hands; the interviewer will probably offer his or her hand first. A **firm** handshake shows confidence (just don't break any fingers!). Look the person directly in the eye with a friendly smile on your face. Don't sit down until the interviewer **offers you a seat**. And make sure you remember to turn off your cell phone! Leaving it on during an interview is a big **no-no,** even if it's set to **vibrate**. (Very often people can hear the vibrating sound. This is almost as bad as letting the phone ring.) We don't even want to think about this, but if you forget to turn the phone off and it rings, **apologize,** and turn the phone off immediately. *Never* answer your phone during a job interview!

Different hiring people have different styles of interviewing job candidates. Some will try to make you feel comfortable, and they may even sit in a chair next to you. Others will sit behind a big desk and have you sit on a small, uncomfortable chair. This can sometimes be intimidating, but the interviewer may just want to see how you handle a situation like this. Don't let it **shake your confidence**!

During the interview, the interviewer may talk about the job and ask you about your experience. But he or she may also ask some tricky questions. For example, a popular job interview question is to ask, "What is your biggest **strength**?" This is a great time to talk about something you've done well in the past. You may say something like, "I think I'm a great **team player**. Even when I'm **in charge**, I know it takes everyone working together to do a great job." The next question may be, "What is your biggest weakness?" This one isn't so easy. It's not a good idea to talk about a real weakness. You'll never get the job if you say, "Well, sometimes it's hard for me to get to work on time." A good idea is to think of something that can actually be a strength. For example, you might say, "I really enjoy helping my co-workers with their projects, so I try to be careful not to take on too many extra **duties**."

Near the end of the interview, the **hiring manager** will probably ask if you have any questions. Make sure that you do! Asking a question about the job shows interest in the position and the company. It's also a chance for you to see if this job is a good fit for you.

## DIALOGUE 2: TRACK 54

**INTERVIEWER:** It's nice to meet you, Alan. I see that you've been with our company for a while now, haven't you? Why are you interested in the supervisor position?

**ALAN:** Well, I've really enjoyed my job so far, but I feel ready to take on more responsibilities. I think I **have a lot to offer** the company.

**INTERVIEWER:** Have you ever had any supervisory experience?

**ALAN:** Well, when my supervisor has a day off, he asks me to help manage the restaurant. That includes supervising the other workers—you know, answering any questions they have, making sure they get their breaks . . . responsibilities like that.

**INTERVIEWER:** Yes, your supervisor **speaks very highly of** you in his letter of recommendation. Well, Alan, can you think of a time when there was a problem you had to **resolve** when you were in charge? And tell us how you managed the situation.

**ALAN:** Well, I can't say I've ever had any problems with my co-workers. But I guess sometimes, if an order wasn't exactly right, a customer might get angry and **nasty**. I just made sure that I stayed calm. I listened politely to his or her complaint, and I redid the order. I always apologized for the mix-up. A lot of times I'd **throw in** a coupon to show **goodwill**. That usually seemed to **do the trick**.

**INTERVIEWER:** Customers can sometimes be tricky. Sounds like you handled those situations very well. It's really important to us that our supervisor is able to deal in a friendly way with customer problems. You probably also know that we're doing more and more work on the computer. Keeping **spreadsheets** is an important part of the job. How are your computer skills? Are you familiar with Excel?

**ALAN:** I do use my home computer a lot, but I haven't needed to use Excel. I'm pretty good at figuring out computer stuff, and I **catch on** pretty quickly, so I'm sure I can **get up to speed** with that program. No problem.

**INTERVIEWER:** Great. Well, do you have any questions for me?

**ALAN:** Yes. I know that the company is growing and opening new locations in different cities. If I'm offered the job, where will I be **based**?

**INTERVIEWER:** Good question. I am glad you reminded me. The position is open in the Eldred location, but we really need someone who can be **flexible.** We'll want this person to **fill in** at our other restaurants when another supervisor is on vacation. Would you be able to do that?

**ALAN:** Absolutely. I'd really enjoy getting to know different locations.

**INTERVIEWER:** Great. Well, Alan, thank you for your time. We'll be **in touch** as soon as we make a decision.

**ALAN:** Thank you for taking the time to talk to me.

---

**TIP 2**

**Interviewers cannot, by law, ask you certain questions. Here are some questions an interviewer is not allowed to ask:**

- What are your religious practices?
- How old are you?
- Where were you born?
- Do you have an illness or disability?
- Are you married?
- Do you have children?

---

**TIP 3**

**Although some of the above questions are not allowed, an interviewer *can* ask the following questions:**

- Are you able to perform all the physical duties of this job?
- After we hire you, can you provide proof that you can work in the United States?
- Will you be able to work during all of the scheduled days and times of this job?

---

## VOCABULARY

- **apologize**: say you're sorry about something
- **based**: have as your main location
- **candidate**: someone being considered for a job
- ⓘ **catch on**: learn
- ⓘ **do the trick**: get a result you want
- ⓘ **dry run**: practice

- **duty**: responsibility, something you have to do
- ⓘ **fill in**: substitute for someone who is not there
- **firm**: strong, but not hard
- **flexible**: able to make changes easily
- ⓘ **get up to speed**: learn what you need to do something
- **goodwill**: friendliness
- ⓘ **have a lot to offer**: be very good at something that can help someone
- **hiring manager**: the person who is in charge of hiring a new employee
- **in charge**: in control
- **intimidating**: making you feel unsure about yourself
- ⓘ **in touch**: be in contact by phone, letter, or e-mail
- **nasty**: mean; unpleasant
- ⓘ **no-no**: something that you cannot do
- **offer someone a seat**: ask someone to sit down
- **panel**: a group of people who will make a decision
- **resolve**: settle; solve
- ⓘ **shake one's confidence**: make you feel unsure about yourself
- **speak highly of**: say very good things about
- **spreadsheets**: a way of keeping information
- **strength**: something you do well
- ⓘ **team player**: someone who works well with others to get a job done
- ⓘ **throw in**: add
- ⓘ **throw you**: make you feel nervous
- **vibrate**: move very fast; shake

## GRAMMAR REMINDER 1: The Present Perfect Simple Tense—Questions

To make a question in the present perfect simple tense, just switch the word order used in an affirmative statement. If needed, add the question word at the beginning.

*Correct Example:*
How long **have you worked** for the company?

*Not:*
How long **you have worked** for the company?

Sometimes we add in the word *ever* for extra emphasis.

**Example:** Have you *ever* had any supervisory experience?

## GRAMMAR REMINDER 2: The Present Perfect Simple Tense—Negatives

Present perfect simple tense negatives are made by adding the word *not* between *have* or *has* and the past participle. (Don't forget those contractions!)

**Example:** I have**n't** needed to use Excel.

## After . . .

It's always a **nerve-racking** time after an interview. You keep thinking about the questions and your answers. How did it go? Why didn't I say *this*? Why didn't I say *that*? You may get a call asking you to come back for a second interview. This is a good sign! It shows that you are one of a few people that they are interested in. They may want you to talk to other people you'll be working with. This is a good time to mention that great thing you forgot in the first interview!

Although a company *should* write or call to let you know if you got the job, not all of them do this. If you **don't hear anything** for a while, it may be that you didn't get the job. It's fine to call the hiring manager and ask if they've made a decision. You can even ask for **feedback** on the interview. Knowing what things went well and what things made them decide to hire someone else can help you prepare for future interviews.

Sometimes, after you've given up all hope, you may get a letter or phone call **out of the blue** offering you that job. We knew you could do it!

## DIALOGUE 3: TRACK 55

**LIA:** Hey, Alan, did you get that supervisor's job?

**ALAN:** I don't know. I haven't heard anything yet, and it's been 10 days now!

**LIA:** Don't worry. Sometimes it can take ages before you hear anything. How do you think it went?

**ALAN:** I think it went okay. I seemed to have most of the **qualities** they were looking for. The only thing is I haven't had much experience with Excel, and that's what they use for all their reports.

**LIA:** Well, that's something you can learn. It's actually pretty easy to work with. I can show you sometime if you'd like. I use it all the time in my job.

**ALAN:** Thanks. I'll **take you up on** that if they offer me the job.

**LIA:** By the way, did you wear your sneakers and jeans?

**ALAN:** No. I took your advice and wore a jacket and tie. Hey, maybe they didn't like my tie!

TIP 4

There are usually a lot of people who interview for each job. You can make yourself **stand out** by looking and sounding professional. You will also stand out if you send an e-mail or short note thanking the interviewer and reminding him or her why you would be such a good choice for the job. You'll also stand out if you have spinach in your teeth. But we don't recommend that!

## VOCABULARY

- ⓘ **don't hear anything**: not receive any information
- • **feedback**: opinions about how you acted in a situation
- • **nerve-racking** (also spelled **nerve-wracking**): very stressful
- ⓘ **out of the blue**: in a very unexpected way
- • **qualities**: things that make you a good worker or person
- ⓘ **stand out**: be noticed
- ⓘ **take someone up on something**: accept someone's invitation to do something

## MORE FUN WITH IDIOMATIC EXPRESSIONS: On the Job

- • **cream of the crop**: the best of the best
  *Our company only interviews the **cream of the crop** from the top universities.*

- • **work like a dog**: work very hard
  *He wanted to make a good impression on his boss, so he **worked like a dog** to finish the report early.*

- • **get the job done**: accomplish what needs to be done

*Mrs. Robinson could always rely on Ramon to **get the job done** when others were having trouble.*

- **all in a day's work**: just a normal part of the job
  *Dealing with angry customers is **all in a day's work** for people who work in the mall.*

- **put your best foot forward**: do your very best at something
  *When you arrive at your new job, it's a good idea to **put your best foot forward** and be helpful and friendly to all your co-workers.*

# Review: Units 19–21

## VOCABULARY

*Fill in the blanks in the paragraph. Use the words below to help you.*

| | | | | |
|---|---|---|---|---|
| reference | interview | downsize | current | let go |
| candidate | strategy | first impressions | skills | walk out |

You have the job of your dreams, but unfortunately the company you work for is forced to (1) _____, and you've been (2) _____. Don't panic. You need to keep a cool head and think of a good (3) _____ to get yourself another job! Don't leave on a bad note and (4) _____ in anger; you may need a (5) _____ from your (6) _____ employer saying why you are such a good (7) _____ for a new position. Practice before going to an (8) _____, especially if it's been a while since you've done this. Make sure they know what (9) _____ you have and remember to dress professionally. (10) _____ are really important!

## INFORMAL LANGUAGE

*Look at how these expressions are used in a sentence. Can you explain what they mean?*

11. Don't worry. I promise I'll keep **in touch** when I move to another state for my new job.

12. Those ladies in the office never seem to do any work! They spend the whole day **yakking** about nothing.

13. I'm afraid my Internet is down, so I'll need to send the documents by **snail mail**.

14. You really should **do your homework** about a company before you decide to work for them.

15. Don't let the cold weather **get you down**. It'll soon be spring.

16. I was really lucky to find that new position **by word of mouth** before it was even posted on the job site.

17. Talking to him is a real **waste of time**. He never listens to my ideas.

18. Once you get your **foot in the door** of a company, you can start to move up.

19. Sometimes in an interview, they will ask tricky questions to try to **throw you**.

20. It is especially important to be a good **team player** in a small company.

## GRAMMAR

*Choose the correct answer from those provided to fill in the gaps.*

**SAMUEL:** Hi, Philip. What's up?

**PHILIP:** Well, there's some good news and some bad news. You know that I (21) **(worked/have worked)** at Jo's café for 10 years now.

**SAMUEL:** Sure. (22) **(Have you decided/Did you decided)** to leave?

**PHILIP:** No. I (23) **(hasn't quit/haven't quit)**. Actually, it's the opposite: I've been offered a promotion.

**SAMUEL:** That's great. Are you going to take them up on their offer?

**PHILIP:** Are you kidding? Of course I am! I'll get paid more, and if I (24) **(will earn/earn)** more money, my wife and I (25) **(will travel/travel)** to see family more often. The bad news is that I'll need that raise to pay off the new fine I owe.

**SAMUEL:** What new fine? (26) **(Did you speed/Were you speeding)** in that fast car of yours again?

**PHILIP:** No. I (27) **(didn't go/wasn't going)** too fast. But I (28) **(did chat/was chatting)** on the cell phone while I (29) **(drived/was driving)**. I was so excited, I couldn't wait to tell my wife. Then the police (30) **(pulled me over/has pulled me over)**.

**SAMUEL:** Oops . . .

**PHILIP:** Yes, oops. Now I've got to go and tell my wife where my first raise is going!

**SAMUEL:** Good luck!

# Answers to Review Activities

## VOCABULARY

1. sale
2. yard
3. platform
4. apply
5. sunroof

6. tricky
7. fare
8. rush hour
9. skip
10. fine

## INFORMAL LANGUAGE

11. **headed**: going
Hi, John. Sorry I can't stop; I'm **headed** to class right now

12. **drive someone nuts**: doing something very annoying (or being annoyed)
My husband never puts the top back on the toothpaste. It's **driving me nuts.**

13. **hang around**: spend time with friends with no special activity, or just wait around
  • I love just **hanging around** with my friends at the mall.
  • I hate hanging **around the doctor's** office, waiting for my turn.

14. **fed up**: tired of something
I'm really **fed up** with getting up at 6 a.m. for my job.

15. **pull over**: move the car to the side of the road
I didn't think I was driving too fast, but the police car's flashing lights meant I should **pull over** anyway.

16. **change your mind**: make a different decision from your first one
I was going to cut my hair really short, but I **changed my mind** because it looks better long.

17. **catch the bus**: get on a bus
I **catch the bus** every morning at 7 a.m.

18. **see the sights**: visit attractions in a new place
   I love to **see the sights** when I visit a new town.

19. **a nightmare**: a very bad situation
   The traffic in this city is **a real nightmare**; there are too many cars.

20. **hail a cab**: signal that you want a taxi
   If you want **to hail a cab**, put out your hand and shout, "Taxi!"

# GRAMMAR

| | |
|---|---|
| 21. b | 26. a |
| 22. d | 27. b |
| 23. c | 28. a |
| 24. c | 29. c |
| 25. c | 30. d |

# Review Answers: Units 4–6

## VOCABULARY

| | |
|---|---|
| 1. vegetarian | 6. spotless |
| 2. cashier | 7. couch potato |
| 3. gourmet | 8. dawn |
| 4. party | 9. sunscreen |
| 5. gadget | 10. sunburn |

## INFORMAL LANGUAGE

11. **d**
   I'd love to buy a new TV to watch the game, but my wife would be angry because it would **break the bank** at the moment.

12. **i**
   My boss always has something **to beef about**. I wish he'd just let me get on with my job in peace.

13. **b**
   Sorry, I can't stop and talk. I want to get home **to catch a game** on TV.

14. **f**
   This new computer program is really easy. It makes writing this report **a piece of cake**.

15. **j**

Morning, everyone! I've brought doughnuts to the office for breakfast. Don't be shy. **Dig in**!

16. **g**

I like **to stay in shape**, so I make sure I exercise regularly and eat lots of fruit and vegetables.

17. **c**

It's fun to play a game of soccer with friends, but sometimes I like to **do my own thing** and go for a jog alone.

18. **h**

If you must go jogging alone, make sure you run in a public place, and **keep an eye open** at all times for problems.

19. **a**

I'm so glad I got my new job. I'm a **happy camper** now!

20. **e**

I hate carrying heavy suitcases. When I go away, I try **to travel light** and take as few things as possible.

# GRAMMAR

✗ 21. Wow, this burger <u>is smelling</u> great.
   *Correct version: This burger **smells** great. (Smell is a stative verb.)*

✗ 22. What would you like: tea or coffee?
   <u>I like coffee.</u>
   *Correct version: **I'd like** coffee. (The question is asking which you **would** like to drink at the moment.)*

✓ 23. *This is correct. (The question is asking what you like in general.)*

✓ 24. *This is correct. (Wine is a noncount noun.)*

✗ 25. Two glasses of wine <u>is</u> very expensive.
   *Correct version: Two glasses of wine **are** very expensive. (Wine is a noncount noun, but here the wine has been poured into **two glasses**. Therefore, the word acts as a count noun.)*

✗ 26. <u>A rice</u> is a good choice with seafood.
   *Correct version: **Rice** is a good choice with seafood. (Rice is a noncount noun, which does not need the indefinite article a.)*

**×**  27. He <u>cans</u> swim well.
*Correct version: He* **can** *swim well. (Can is a modal verb and is followed by a verb in its base form.)*

**×**  28. I <u>can played</u> soccer well when I was younger.
*Correct version: I* **could play** *soccer well when I was young. (The past of* can *is* could, *followed by a verb in the base form.)*

**✓**  29. *This is correct. (Pour is a regular verb, so it takes* ed *as its ending.)*

**×**  30. I loved my teacher in first grade. She <u>teached me</u> many wonderful things.
*Correct version: I loved my teacher in first grade. She* **taught** *me many wonderful things. (The verb* to teach *is an irregular verb; the past tense is* taught.)

# Review Answers: Units 7–9

## VOCABULARY

| | |
|---|---|
| 1. f | 11. relocating |
| 2. j | 12. settle down |
| 3. e | 13. appliances |
| 4. h | 14. junk mail |
| 5. i | 15. direct deposit |
| 6. d | 16. denominations |
| 7. b | 17. stereotype |
| 8. a | 18. stroller |
| 9. c | 19. bargains |
| 10. g | 20. rain check |

## INFORMAL LANGUAGE

21. **out of luck**: don't have a chance
Sorry Alfredo, it's not going to happen!

22. **off the hook**: not held responsible for something
I will not hold you responsible for coming in late—*this time!*

23. **get away from it all**: leave responsibilities and relax
I need to take a vacation and not think about work!

24. **big bucks**: a lot of money
    Fred must be earning a lot of money to buy such a beautiful new car!

25. **money to burn**: have a lot of extra money
    You must have a lot of extra money because it costs a lot to go on vacation—*especially* more than one time!

26. **takes some getting used to**: need to become accustomed to
    It may take you some time to start enjoying life in the country if you lived in the city before.

27. **look like a million bucks**: look GREAT!
    Julia, you look great in that beautiful dress!

28. **chunk of change**: large amount of money
    The meal cost me a large amount of money.

29. **headache**: something complicated and annoying
    Driving through the city is really hard, because it is so large and it takes so long!

30. **slapped with**: charged for
    We'll get a huge phone bill, because you spend so much time talking!

# GRAMMAR

**CARRIE:** Hi, Mike. Did you <u>enjoyed</u> your vacation?

**MIKE:** Vacation? It <u>weren't</u> a vacation. Everything possible went wrong.

**CARRIE:** Did it <u>rained</u>?

**MIKE:** Yes, it rained all the time. I spent most of the time drinking coffee in cafés!

**CARRIE:** Did you <u>visited</u> many places?

**MIKE:** No, I didn't <u>went</u> anywhere. It was just too awful to go out. We <u>wasn't</u> happy campers.

**CARRIE:** Well, was it a nice hotel?

**MIKE:** No, it was really old and very expensive.

**CARRIE:** How <u>many</u> money did you <u>paid</u>?

**MIKE:** You don't want to know. Way too much! The only good thing is I spent <u>fewer</u> money than if we <u>was</u> able to go out!

## They should say:

**CARRIE:** Hi, Mike. Did you **enjoy** your vacation?

**MIKE:** Vacation? It **wasn't** a vacation. Everything possible went wrong.

**CARRIE:** Did it **rain**?

**MIKE:** Yes, it rained all the time. I spent most of the time drinking coffee in cafés!

**CARRIE:** Did you **visit** many places?

**MIKE:** No, I didn't **go** anywhere. It was just too awful to go out. We **weren't** happy campers.

**CARRIE:** Well, was it a nice hotel?

**MIKE:** No, it was really old and very expensive.

**CARRIE:** How **much** money did you **pay**?

**MIKE:** You don't want to know. Way too much! The only good thing is I spent **less** money than if we **were** able to go out!

# Review Answers: Units 10–12

## VOCABULARY

| | |
|---|---|
| 1. victim | 6. ache |
| 2. unconscious | 7. co-pay |
| 3. witness | 8. poke |
| 4. symptoms | 9. root canal |
| 5. sneeze | 10. dilate |

## INFORMAL LANGUAGE

11. I thought the new job would be better than the old one, but actually it was out of the **frying** pan and into the fire.
    My new job was worse than the old one.

12. Poor Aunt Hilda is in bad **shape** after falling and breaking her arm. I should go and visit her tomorrow.
    Aunt Hilda is in very bad health after her accident.

13. You look the **picture of health** after your vacation in the Caribbean!
    You look so healthy after your vacation.

14. I love getting new projects at work, especially interesting ones that I can really **sink** my teeth into.
I love projects that make me excited

15. He was so lucky to survive the accident. He escaped by the **skin** of his teeth.
It was a serious accident but he got out just in time.

16. It's wonderful to see you after such a long time. You're a **sight** for sore eyes!
It makes me really happy to see you after so long.

17. His mother turned a **blind** eye when her son pretended he was doing his homework while he played on the computer.
His mother knew he was playing on the computer but she pretended he was working.

18. Poor Tony. After he ate that huge Thanksgiving meal he was as sick as a **dog**.
His stomach was so upset that Tony was very sick.

19. It's no good. I just don't understand these computers. I guess you just can't teach an old dog new **tricks**!
I'm so used to doing things the old way that this new system is too hard for me to learn.

20. The neighbor's kids are so noisy. They fight like **cats** and dogs all the time.The kids fight or argue a lot.

## GRAMMAR

21. have to (shows that something is necessary)

22. should (strong advice)

23. could (a polite way to request something)

24. should (strong advice)

25. don't have to (something is not necessary)

26. have to (The word *will* shows this is something necessary in the future, so you need to use the phrase *have to*.)

27. had to (something was necessary in the past)

28. could (used for past ability)

29. would (to express what you might do in a certain situation)

30. could (expresses possibility)

# Review Answers: Units 13–15

## VOCABULARY

1. reliable

2. gossip

3. hobby

4. pothole

5. litter

6. amateur

7. paparazzi

8. bugs

9. fragile

10. knit

## INFORMAL LANGUAGE

11. **scope out**: explore; find out about things
    Before their camping trip, they **scoped out** places to put their tent.

12. **give someone a hand**: help someone
    John **gave the old lady a hand** carrying her heavy bags to her car.

13. **grab a quick bite**: have a quick, casual small meal or snack
    Sue **grabbed a quick bite** between classes.

14. **keep an eye on**: watch in a protective way
    The mother **kept an eye** on her children at the park.

15. **pricey**: expensive
    The designer bag was too **pricey**, so she didn't buy it.

16. **catch up**: learn all the news from someone
    They hadn't seen each other in a long time, so it was great to **catch up**.

17. **treat to**: pay for as a special event or reward
    The kid was so well behaved that his mom **treated him to** ice cream after dinner.

18. **dying to**: want to do something very much
    They were **dying to** see the popular new movie on Saturday night.

19. **Plan B**: a second-choice plan
    The movie was sold out, so they went to **Plan B** and saw a different film.

20. **running behind**: late
The bus was late, so she was **running behind** for her meeting.

## GRAMMAR

21. between

22. in

23. on

24. in

25. near

✗ 26. I'm <u>not wanting</u> fries with my burger.
*Correct version: I **don't want** fries with my burger. (**Want** is a stative verb and is not used in the continuous form.)*

✗ 27. <u>I meet</u> some friends this afternoon.
*Correct version: I **am meeting** some friends this afternoon. (You need to use the present continuous tense to show something that will happen in the near future. You could also use going to here to show a plan. I **am going to meet** some friends this afternoon.)*

✗ 28. <u>We read</u> a really good book at our book club this month.
*Correct version: We **are reading** a really good book at our book club this month. (You need to use the present continuous tense to show an action happening now.)*

✗ 29. <u>You are meeting</u> your friends this afternoon?
*Correct version: **Are you meeting** your friends this afternoon? (You need to reverse the word order to show a question.)*

✓ 30. No errors

# Review Answers: Units 16–18

## VOCABULARY

1. propose

2. stroll

3. elope

4. pack

5. cringe

6. soothe

7. overdo

8. choked

9. dribble

10. crawl

# INFORMAL LANGUAGE

11. **e**
    John, you are terrible! Every pretty girl who walks by **catches your eye**.

12. **h**
    The first time I saw my wife, I **chatted her up** because I was sure she was someone special.

13. **j**
    I always look forward to going out on a Friday night so I can **let my hair down** and have fun after a busy week.

14. **g**
    Have you heard the news? Toby and Ann are going to **tie the knot** at last!

15. **i**
    Let's all **chip in** together to buy a really nice gift for Fiona's new baby.

16. **a**
    OK, I'm **all ears**. I just can't wait to hear about your new boyfriend!

17. f
    Alan, you really **look down** today. What's going on?

18. **d**
    It's going to be a tough match against the All Stars, but I want everyone to **give it their best shot**. We can win if we try our hardest!

19. **b**
    Have you heard? Janet is **eating for two** now. The baby is due in November.

20. **c**
    My daughter and I both wear glasses. It **runs in the family.**

## GRAMMAR: Phrasal Verbs

21. **go out**: meet and spend time with someone

22. **let someone down**: disappoint someone

23. **make up**: forgive and be friends again

24. **put up with**: have patience to ignore something annoying

25. **split up**: separate; no longer be together

## GRAMMAR: *Will* or *Going To*

26. is going to (The black clouds indicate something you can see is definitely going to happen.)

27. am going to (This is something you have already decided.)

28. will (This indicates a decision made right now.)

29. will (It's a fact!)

30. are going to (This is something you have already decided.)

# Review Answers: Units 19–21

## VOCABULARY

| | |
|---|---|
| 1. downsize | 6. current |
| 2. let go | 7. candidate |
| 3. strategy | 8. interview |
| 4. walk out | 9. skills |
| 5. reference | 10. first impressions |

## INFORMAL LANGUAGE

11. **in touch**: connected by talking or writing
I promise I'll phone, write, or e-mail you.

12. **yak**: have a very casual conversation, usually about nothing
They spend the whole day talking about nothing.

13. **snail mail**: the postal service
I'll have to send them in the regular post, not by e-mail.

14. **do your homework**: look carefully to find out about something
You need to find out as much as you can about this company.

15. **get you down**: make you feel discouraged
Don't let the cold weather depress you. It will soon get warm.

16. **word of mouth**: hearing something from a friend
A friend told me about the job before it was posted.

17. **waste of time**: something that is not worth doing
There is no point talking to him because he doesn't listen.

18. **foot in the door**: first step in working toward a goal
When you start to work in a place, even in a low-level position, it is a good start that could help you get a better position someday.

19. **throw you**: make you feel nervous
Sometimes they will ask difficult questions to see if you can answer them under stress.

20. **team player**: someone who works well with others to get a job done
You need to be able to work well with others in a small company.

## GRAMMAR

21. have worked

22. have you decided

23. haven't quit

24. earn

25. will travel

26. were you speeding

27. wasn't going

28. was chatting

29. was driving

30. pulled me over

# Appendix A
## AUDIO CD TRACKS

| CD Track | Unit | Dialogue | Transcript |
|---|---|---|---|
| 1 | | | Title and Intro |
| 2 | 1 | 1 | Hi There! |
| 3 | 1 | 2 | Meet the Neighbors |
| 4 | 1 | 3 | Those Crazy Kids! |
| 5 | 2 | 1 | Riding the Bus |
| 6 | 2 | 2 | Going Underground: The Subway |
| 7 | 2 | 3 | Hey, Taxi |
| 8 | 3 | 1 | Everybody Loves the DMV |
| 9 | 3 | 2 | Let's Go for a Ride! |
| 10 | 3 | 3 | Oops. Sorry, Officer |
| 11 | 4 | 1 | Zipping Through the Drive-Thru |
| 12 | 4 | 2 | A Little More Upscale |
| 13 | 4 | 3 | Is This What I Ordered? |
| 14 | 5 | 1 | Play Ball! |
| 15 | 5 | 2 | Members Only! Joining a Gym |
| 16 | 5 | 3 | Extreme Sports |
| 17 | 6 | 1 | Day Tripping |
| 18 | 6 | 2 | Going Wild |
| 19 | 6 | 3 | Fancy-Schmancy |
| 20 | 7 | 1 | To Buy or Not to Buy; That Is the Question |
| 21 | 7 | 2 | City Life or the 'Burbs |
| 22 | 7 | 3 | Nothing but Bills! |
| 23 | 8 | 1 | Stash the Cash! Get Started with Banking |
| 24 | 8 | 2 | Making the Big Bucks |
| 25 | 9 | 1 | It's All at the Mall |
| 26 | 9 | 2 | Food, Glorious Food! |
| 27 | 9 | 3 | Saving Some Dough |
| 28 | 10 | 1 | HELP! FIRE! |
| 29 | 10 | 2 | HELP! HE'S NOT BREATHING! |
| 30 | 10 | 3 | HELP! STRANGER DANGER! |

# Appendix A
## (continued)
## AUDIO CD TRACKS

| CD Track | Unit | Dialogue | Transcript |
|---|---|---|---|
| 31 | 11 | 1 | Under the Weather |
| 32 | 11 | 2 | Health Insurance: What's Up with That? |
| 33 | 12 | 1 | Open Wide |
| 34 | 12 | 2 | Let's See |
| 35 | 12 | 3 | WOOF! |
| 36 | 13 | 1 | Where Am I? |
| 37 | 13 | 2 | At Your Service |
| 38 | 14 | 1 | What's Happening? |
| 39 | 14 | 2 | See the Capital . . . and the Capitol |
| 40 | 15 | 1 | Helping Hands, Giving Back |
| 41 | 15 | 2 | Good Citizen? Good Neighbor! |
| 42 | 16 | 1 | The Dating Game |
| 43 | 16 | 2 | Will You Marry Me? |
| 44 | 16 | 3 | It's Over! |
| 45 | 17 | 1 | And Baby Makes Three |
| 46 | 17 | 2 | That Bundle of Joy |
| 47 | 18 | 1 | End-of-Life Issues |
| 48 | 18 | 2 | Funeral Customs |
| 49 | 19 | 1 | Hello? Hello? Can You Hear Me Now? |
| 50 | 19 | 2 | The Easy Way |
| 51 | 20 | 1 | The Perfect Job |
| 52 | 20 | 2 | Paperwork! |
| 53 | 21 | 1 | Before . . . |
| 54 | 21 | 2 | During . . . |
| 55 | 21 | 3 | After . . . |

# Appendix B

## COMMON IRREGULAR VERBS

| Base Form | Simple Past | Past Participle |
|---|---|---|
| be | was/were | been |
| beat | beat | beat |
| become | became | become |
| begin | began | begun |
| bet | bet | bet |
| bite | bit | bitten |
| blow | blew | blown |
| break | broke | broken |
| bring | brought | brought |
| build | built | built |
| buy | bought | bought |
| catch | caught | caught |
| choose | chose | chosen |
| come | came | come |
| cost | cost | cost |
| cut | cut | cut |
| do | did | done |
| draw | drew | drawn |
| drink | drank | drunk |
| drive | drove | driven |
| eat | ate | eaten |
| fall | fell | fallen |
| fight | fought | fought |
| find | found | found |
| fit | fit | fit |
| fly | flew | flown |
| forget | forgot | forgotten |
| forgive | forgave | forgiven |
| get | got | gotten/got |

| Base Form | Simple Past | Past Participle |
|---|---|---|
| give | gave | given |
| go | went | gone |
| grow | grew | grown |
| have | had | had |
| hear | heard | heard |
| hide | hid | hidden |
| hurt | hurt | hurt |
| keep | kept | kept |
| know | knew | known |
| leave | left | left |
| let | let | let |
| lose | lost | lost |
| make | made | made |
| meet | met | met |
| pay | paid | paid |
| put | put | put |
| quit | quit | quit |
| read (pronounced "reed") | read (pronounced "red") | read (pronounced "red") |
| ride | rode | ridden |
| ring | rang | rung |
| run | ran | run |
| say | said | said |
| see | saw | seen |
| sell | sold | sold |
| send | sent | sent |
| set | set | set |
| shake | shook | shaken |

# Appendix B

(continued)

## COMMON IRREGULAR VERBS

| Base Form | Simple Past | Past Participle |
|-----------|-------------|-----------------|
| show | showed | shown |
| sing | sang | sung |
| sit | sat | sat |
| sleep | slept | slept |
| speak | spoke | spoken |
| split | split | split |
| stand | stood | stood |
| steal | stole | stolen |
| stick | stuck | stuck |
| swim | swam | swum |
| take | took | taken |
| teach | taught | taught |
| tell | told | told |
| think | thought | thought |
| throw | threw | thrown |
| understand | understood | understood |
| wake | woke | woken |
| win | won | won |
| write | wrote | written |

# Appendix C

## VOCABULARY

**A**

ablaze, 168
absolutely, 37, 120
a bunch, 7
access, 109
accomplishments, 220
accurately, 180
ache, 106
achy, 106
acknowledging, 155
acronym, 207
ad, 83
additions, 128
add up, 128
adorable, 185
advance, 55
advance notice, 65
adventurous streak, 48
afford, 140
affordable, 214
ages, 214
aggressive, 134
aisle, 86
a little while, 110
all ears, 168
all I know is, 102
all-inclusive, 57
allowed, 23
all sorts of, 46
all your ducks in a row, 214
amateur, 140
amazed, 128
amenities, 57
Americanize, 220
anchor store, 83
animal control officer, 134
anniversary, 168
annual fee, 46
answer, 203
anything and everything, 191
apartment complexes, 128
apologize, 37, 229
apparent, 185
appetizer, 34

appliances, 65
application, 203, 214
apply, 18
arcade, 57
architecture, 145
arm candy, 163
arrange, 15
art form, 220
artificial, 86
arts groups, 140
ashes, 195
assets, 151
at home, 128
ATM, 75
attractions, 48
audiobooks, 128
audition, 140
avenue, 128
avoiding, 180
awesome, 57

**B**

baby-proofed, 185
baby shower, 185
bachelor, 168
bachelorette, 168
backstroke, 37
bad day, 37
bad hair days, 18
bad news, 18
bad rap, 30
bagel, 168
bait, 55
balance, 75
balancing, 151
ban, 203
barbecue, 5, 163
bargain, 89
barking, 5
based, 229
basil, 86
beats, 168
beautiful, 220

catch up, 140
catch you later, 7
cat people, 134
caught fire, 97
CD, 75
cell phone, 97
cemetery, 195
central location, 128
change, 78
change your mind, 5
chaplain, 191
charity, 195
chart, 109
chartering, 57
chat, 23
chatting someone up, 163
cheating on, 172
check, 78
checked in, 128
checked out, 106
check in, 34
checking, 75
check out, 46, 128
checkup, 114
chicken, 48
chicken nuggets, 30
chillin', 7
chilly, 19
chip in together, 169
choking, 169
chronic, 191
chunk, 114
chunk of change, 65
cinema, 140
city person, 68
classifieds, 214
cleaning, 114
C-note, 78
cocktails, 163
code enforcement people, 128
coffin, 195
colic, 185
come across, 225
comes with the territory, 155
comfy, 114
committed, 120
communication, 203
commuter, 10, 128
compact, 21

compensation package, 214
competitively, 42
complex, 145
complicated, 10
compliment, 86
compliments of the house, 37
compose, 207
concerned, 118
concession stand, 42
concierge, 58
concourse, 145
condition, 109
condolences, 195
confident, 225
confusing, 134
congressional representative, 145
conscious, 100
conscious of, 30
conservative, 225
consider, 65
contractions, 180
contribution, 155
convenient, 19, 180
convertible, 21
convince, 214
cooped up, 185
cop, 23
co-pay, 109
corner, 128
correct, 37
couch, 140
couch potato, 43
cougars, 163
counseling, 172
counselor, 58
count me in, 48, 128
count me out, 48
count on, 172
country, 21, 68
coupon, 89
cover, 109
cover letter, 220
CPR, 100
crafts, 86, 134
crawling, 185
crazy, 7
crazy about, 13
creamy, 86
creature, 120

hands-on, 180
handwritten, 207
handy, 65
hanging around, 19
hang out, 2
hang up, 97
hard-won, 155
hassle, 75
hatchback, 21
have a lot to offer, 230
have something checked out, 115
having an affair, 172
HDTV, 207
headache, 68
headed, 2
headhunters, 215
headlights, 195
head office, 225
health conscious, 31
health history, 110
health insurance, 110
health plan, 107
heavy rain, 134
he can really move, 43
heck, 43
hectic, 2
helping out, 151
hen, 169
herbs, 86
hey, 3
hi, 3
hidden extras, 53
high-class, 58
hilarious, 164
hint, 43
hip, 121
hiring manager, 230
hobby, 128
hogging, 43
hold, 34
homebound shut-ins, 151
homegrown, 86
homeless shelter, 152
homemade, 86
honeymoon, 169
honor, 152
hookup, 65
hook up, 207
hop into, 31

hop on, 13
hospice care, 192
hospitalization, 110
host, 5
hostess station, 34
hot air balloon, 48
hours, 140
housewares, 83
housewarming, 70
house wine, 34
how come, 215
how would you like it?, 34
HR, 215
huge, 3
hum, 207
humanely, 134
Human Resources, 215
human resources department, 110
husk, 86
hygienist, 115

I
ice cream cone, 121
ID, 75
I do, 169
I have no idea, 102
ill, 110
illegal, 203
I'm afraid, 115
immediately, 37
immunizations, 134
in advance, 15, 58
in a flash, 185
in ages, 186
in charge, 230
incision, 180
included, 215
incurable, 192
infant, 186
infected, 115
in heaven, 58
injury, 121
in-laws, 169
in lieu of, 195
in person, 23, 140
insider scoop, 140
instant, 207
instruments, 115
insufficient, 128

make a right, 128
make-believe, 169
make no sense, 78
make up, 173
making arrangements, 195
mall, 3
mandatory, 134
manufacturer, 89
mass transit, 11
matter of life and death, 97
mayo, 31
M.D., 118
Meals-on-Wheels, 152
meaning to do something, 5
medication, 110, 115
medicine, 110
memorials, 146
memorial service, 195
mention, 37
mentioned, 86
merchandise, 215
middle of nowhere, 56
midsize, 21
midwife, 180
mind, 83
minimum, 75
mint, 78
miss, 129
missing, 134
mix-up, 37
mock, 225
molar, 115
mom-to-be, 180
monuments, 146
mooing and clucking, 68
morning sickness, 180
mountain lions, 163
movie times, 141
moving violation, 23
Mr. or Ms. Right, 164
multiplex, 164
multi-tap, 204
municipal building, 129
Murphy's Law, 71
music releases, 141
mutt, 134

**N**
nachos, 43

nail, 225
name brand, 110
nap, 48
Napa Valley, 34
nasty, 230
natural, 225
nature, 100
nature paths, 134
nerve-racking, 180, 232
network, 110
neutered, 134
new arrival, 180
newborn, 186
next door, 5
nickel, 78
nightmare, 15
night out, 186
9 to 5, 215
no kidding, 78
no-no, 230
not buying, 115
notice, 23, 155
nowadays, 180
nuke, 66
nursing home, 152
nutrients, 186
nutrition, 186

**O**
OB/GYN, 180
obituary, 195
observe, 204
offend, 115
offer someone a seat, 230
officer, 23
off the hook, 65
oh, come on, 115
OJ, 34
old-fashioned, 169
once, 129
on display, 146
on draft, 34
one of the family, 121
onesies, 186
only have eyes for someone, 169
on my way, 129
onomatopoeia, 68
on one's own, 192
on sale, 89

snail mail, 207
sneezing, 107
sniffing, 207
snowstorm, 207
snuggled, 121
soothe, 186
sore, 107
soup kitchen, 152
source, 207
sources, 164
souvenir, 58, 83
spa, 58
spayed, 135
speak highly of, 230
speaking of, 79
special exhibition, 141
specialized, 110
specialty store, 83
specific, 69
specifically, 110
spectacular, 53
speeding, 23
speedy, 129
split the gas, 146
split up, 173
splurge, 35
spotless, 38, 186
spouse, 173
spread out, 58
spreadsheets, 230
squeeze someone in, 107
stadium, 43
staff member, 110
stag, 170
staged, 226
stages of labor, 181
stamps, 129
stand out, 232
star, 152
Stars and Stripes, 129
starting a family, 181
stash, 75
state trooper, 23
staycation, 53
stay connected, 152
stay in shape, 46
stay tuned, 13
steal, 89
stepparents, 170

stepped up to the plate, 155
stereotype, 83
stiff, 121, 129
Story Hour, 129
strategy, 226
stray, 135
strength, 230
stress, 118
strip mall, 83
stroll, 164
stroller, 83
stuck with, 19
stuff, 46
stuffy nose, 107
stunner, 164
stylin', 7
submitting, 216
substitute, 110
suburbs, 5
subway, 11
sugar daddy, 164
suit any pocketbook, 53
suite, 58
suit jacket, 226
sunburn, 53
sunroof, 21
sunscreen, 53
supervise, 192
supervisor, 220
support system, 192
surf, 53
surgery, 181
sympathy, 196
symptoms, 107

**T**

taboo, 196
tags, 204
tail, 121
take advantage of, 155
take forever, 66
take for granted, 155
takeout, 31
takes me back, 170
take some getting used to, 79
take someone up on something, 232
take the bus or train, 11
talent, 152
tame, 49

victim, 98
viewing, 196
vision test, 19
visit, 181
visiting times, 196
vital, 97
vital signs, 110
vocal, 181
voice mail, 204
volunteerism, 152
voting district, 146

**W**
wacky, 14
wags, 121
wake, 196
walk out, 216
warning, 207
wassup, 7
waste of time, 221
watch one's weight, 43
way too many/much, 216
wealthy, 121
weapon, 102
we'd better, 115
wedded bliss, 173
wedding planner, 170
weigh one's options, 66
weird, 115
what're you up to, 7
where on earth, 226
whining, 186
whirlwind, 170
white picket fence, 66
whitewater rafting, 49
whole bunch, 46
whole grains, 31
will, 121
window-shopping, 83
windshield, 35
within walking distance, 69
witness, 100
wondering, 186
word of mouth, 216
work out, 46
work things out, 173
worth, 221
write home, 129
written test, 19

**Y**
yak, 204
yards, 5
yoga, 135
you can't miss it, 129
you're on your own, 66
your loss, 49
YouTube, 207

**Z**
zap, 66
zipline, 49
zoning requirements, 130

# Notes

# Notes

# Notes

# Notes

# How to Use the Audio
## Listen Everywhere!

**CD**—Listen to the audio CD at home, pop it into your car stereo, or play it on your computer at work. (Oops. Where's the boss?) The CD contains all the dialogues (Appendix A has each dialogue and track number), so you can listen along as you read. It's a great tool to help you improve your own pronunciation.

**Mp3 Files**—Perfect for all your mobile devices. Head to *http://www.rea.com/etaw* for the audio content. After a quick download of the Mp3 files (follow your media player's guide for instructions), you can hear all of the dialogues and pronunciation pointers. Practice, practice, practice!

As you listen, pay special attention to the way the speakers… well, speak. You'll notice that words and phrases join together, rather than always being pronounced as separate sounds. Stop the audio as you listen, and try to copy the rhythm and stress of the speakers. You'll find that your own pronunciation will improve.

You know what we say in English: Practice makes perfect. Have fun!